THE SIMPLE

VEGAN

COOKBOOK

100 Healthy, Foolproof and Frugal Plant-based Vegan

Recipes You Love Forever

By Morrisa Angela

CONTENT

Foreword

Have you heard the good news?

There is a lifestyle that can help you lose weight, make your body healthier overall, save millions of animals, and cause less destruction to the planet. I'm talking about veganism! Millions of people all over the world are switching to a plant-based diet and in this book, you will find out why. Not only that, you'll also receive 100 vegan recipes that are easy to prepare, absolutely delicious, and healthy for your body.

Use this book as your guide to a healthy vegan lifestyle. You can start by reading the helpful and informative explanation of veganism or you can skip to the detailed introduction to vegan foods and the common mistakes you will want to avoid as you transition to a vegan diet. Whenever you're ready, dive into the recipes! You'll love the selection of delicious dishes, from sweet and savory breakfasts, to satisfying soups and stews, mouthwatering main dishes, party pleasing side dishes and appetizers, dressings and sauces to jazz up any dish, and salads and snacks for those times when you just need a little munch!

Refer to this guide whenever you have a question, if you need a little motivation, or when you want to easily make a scrumptious plant-based dish for yourself, friends, family, or special guests. We hope that this book makes your transition to veganism as smooth as possible. And if you're not looking to go vegan yet, we hope that you try these recipes and enjoy the robust and satisfying flavors until you're ready to make the switch. So go ahead, turn the page and start your journey! Enjoy!

PART I Transitioning to a Vegan Diet

A Short History of Veganism

"The Gods created certain kinds of beings to replenish our bodies; they are the trees and the plants and the seeds." – Plato (428-347 BC)

      Veganism is not a new concept to our world. While the recent explosion in the popularity of veganism and a plant-based lifestyle may seem like a recent phenomenon, this practice has roots that date back to more than 2,000 years ago. Many Greek philosophers like Pythagoras, Socrates, Hippocrates, and Plato praised the consumption of plants over the destruction of animal lives for food. Some argue that the history of rejecting the consumption of animals in any form even predates recorded history. There are many cultures around the world that subsisted on fruits, nuts, and vegetables for centuries prior to incorporating meat into their diets. The reason for introducing animals as food is largely unknown, however, it is speculated that poor growing conditions, a nomadic lifestyle, and colonialism could all be possible explanations for the change in diet in communities that did not eat meat for centuries.

What is Veganism?

The term "vegan" wasn't coined until 1944 when Donald Watson, a non-dairy vegetarian, decided that there should be an easier and more encompassing way to identify the type of vegetarian diet that he and many of his friends and colleagues followed. So, he took the first three and the last two letters from the word vegetarian and created the term vegan as a way to describe the rejection of animal flesh and byproducts as food.

What is the difference between veganism and vegetarianism, anyway? Well, the simple answer is that a vegan is a type of vegetarian, restricting the use of animal products completely. However, there are many types of vegetarians:

- Lacto-ovo Vegetarian (most common): Does not eat meat, fish, poultry, or any animal flesh of any kind. They do consume eggs and dairy.
- Lacto Vegetarian: Does not eat eggs, meat, fish, poultry, or any animal flesh of any kind. They do consume dairy.
- Ovo Vegetarian: Does not eat dairy, meat, fish, poultry, or any animal flesh of any kind. They do consume eggs.
- Pescatarian*: Does not eat meat, or poultry. They do consume fish and seafood and may also consume eggs and/or dairy.
- Flexitarian*: Generally, follows a vegetarian diet but may consume a meat dish on occasion.   They make an effort to eat as few animal products as possible.
- Vegan: Does not eat eggs, dairy, honey, meat, fish, poultry, or any animal flesh of any kind.
  It is argued that these are not technically vegetarians, however, these diets are often considered in conversations on vegetarianism, so they have been included here.

A vegan diet *is* a vegetarian diet, with additional restrictions. Most vegetarians follow a lacto-ovo lifestyle so when you go to a restaurant and order a vegetarian meal it is likely to be made with eggs or include dairy of some sort, most commonly cheese. For example, a vegetarian burger might be made with egg to bind the ingredients together and topped with a slice of pepper jack cheese. A vegan burger, on the other hand, would be made with flax seeds to bind the ingredients together and would be served sans cheese and instead topped with a vegan sauce like avocado lime or spicy cashew. Yum!

Why Do People Go Vegan?

Veganism is about more than just restricting the use of animal products. For many following the lifestyle, the practice has a much deeper meaning. Veganism is often broken down into three categories when discussing the "why are you a vegan?" question.   Here is a short explanation of each.

Ethical: Ethical vegans are strongly against the exploitation of animals in any way. They believe that it is wrong to mass produce animals for human consumption whether it be to eat them, wear their skin as leather, or wear their fur as coats. Ethical vegans also think it is wrong to repeatedly impregnate animals to force the production of milk. This practice takes a heavy toll on the mother cow physically and often the male calf is either killed immediately after birth or raised for a few months, then killed and turned into veal. Meanwhile, the female calf is raised to face the same treatment as her mother. Additionally, ethical vegans do not wear leather, fur, wool, silk, or down filled coats. Many ethical vegans are self-proclaimed animal lovers and they are vegan "for the animals."

Environmental: Environmental vegans refrain from consuming animal products to lessen their carbon foot print. Factory farming has a huge impact on methane emissions, deforestation, water usage (which has caused droughts in many parts of the world), water pollution, and air pollution. In addition, the animal waste that runs off from the farms puts surrounding communities at risk for serious health issues as many of the animals fall sick while being raised in this manner. Their bodies and/or fecal matter often become incorporated into the waste run off that eventually contaminates the water supply. Factory farming is the 2nd highest source of greenhouse gas emissions and produces more of it than all transportation of all kinds combined. Environmental vegans seek to reduce their participation in climate change and global warming. They are vegan "for the environment."

Health: Many vegans choose a plant-based diet because it is better for their health. The leading cause of death in the United States is heart disease. The leading cause of heart disease is plaque buildup in the arteries which is directly related to lifestyle choices i.e., diet and exercise. Dr. Caldwell Esselstyn, Dr. Baxter Montgomery, Dr. Kim Williams, and Dr. Dean Ornish have all claimed to reverse (cure) heart disease in their patients with a vegan diet. In other cases, vegans have reversed diabetes, high blood pressure and other auto immune diseases by excluding meat, dairy, and eggs. Additionally, vegans report better sleep, glowing skin, weight loss, a better mood and a general sense of well-being as side effects to the vegan diet.

Vegan Foods-The Vegan Pantry (Vegan vs. Non-vegan)

So what can I eat on a vegan diet? That's a great question! We'll actually start with the items that you can't eat because, believe it or not, it's a shorter list. The Standard American Diet is so narrow that we often eat many of the same foods week in and week out, hardly realizing that there is an abundance of fruits and vegetables in a variety of preparations to eat and enjoy.

Stay away from these items:
Animal flesh
- o Red Meat
- o White Meat
- o Fish/Seafood
- o Poultry/Fowl

Animal byproducts

- o Eggs
  - • Mayonnaise
- o Dairy
  - • Milk, Butter, Cream, Cheese
- o Stocks or soup bases made with animal bones
- o Gelatin
  - • Jell-O and some candies
- o Sugar that has been refined with animal bones
- o Wine, beer, and alcohol that has been refined with animal bones

<u>Eat these items in variety and abundance:</u>

Fruit

- o Berries
  - • Strawberries, raspberries, blueberries, blackberries, acai, cranberry, currant, goji, persimmon, etc.
- o Citrus
  - • Grapefruit, oranges, limes, pomelo, bitter orange, tangerine, Ugli fruit, lemons, key lime, blood orange, etc.
- o Melons
  - • Watermelon, cantaloupe, honeydew, autumn sweet, sky rocket, etc.
- o Stone Fruits
  - • Peaches, apricots, cherries, plums, etc.
- o General Fruits
  - • Mango, pineapple, apple, banana, tomatoes, grapes etc.

Vegetables

- o Greens
  - • Lettuce (all varieties), spinach, Swiss chard, rainbow chard, etc.
- o Cruciferous Vegetables

- Kale, cauliflower, Brussels sprouts, rocket (arugula), collard greens, cabbage, broccoli, Romanesco, bok choy, mustard greens, watercress, radish, etc.
  - Root Vegetables/Squash
    - Potatoes, sweet potatoes, rutabaga, jicama, parsnips, carrots, cassava, celery, turnips, ginger, onion, etc.
    - Pumpkin, butternut squash, yellow squash, zucchini, acorn squash, spaghetti squash, etc.

Beans/Legumes/Grains/Nuts/Seeds
- Beans/Legumes
  - Black beans, red beans, white beans, chickpeas, kidney beans, black eyed peas, peas, lima beans, lentils, etc.
  - Peanuts
- Grains
  - Rice, barley, kamut, teff, wheat, rye, millet, corn, etc.
  - Amaranth, buckwheat, quinoa (not technically grains, considered pseudo cereals but categorized as grains)
- Nuts/Seeds
  - Almonds, cashews, walnuts, pecans, brazil nuts, hazelnut, macadamia, chestnut, pistachios, etc.
  - Pumpkin seeds, sesame seeds, sunflower seeds,

As you can see there is no shortage to what you can eat on a vegan diet. The list provided isn't even comprehensive! There are so any different types of fruits and vegetables from all over the world. You'll never run out of things to eat as long as you remember that there is actually more that you *can* eat compared to what you can't anymore. The most important thing is changing your mindset on what a meal looks like. Once you reframe your mind, everything will fall into place.

Gradually Going Vegan

The best way to go vegan is the way that works best for you! What is the point of doing something that you aren't able to maintain and that doesn't make you happy? Our recommendation is to start off by trying vegan a few foods. Next time you are out at a restaurant, and they have a vegan option, order it! If you like it, great! If you don't ok, now you know that you don't like that particular type of vegan food. A sad, hard truth is that, in the beginning, you may eat some foods that you just don't like. You'll be trying so many new and different recipes and menu items that, of course, you'll run into the occasional dud. It's happened to every vegan and guess what? We are all still alive and still vegan!

Next, add foods into your diet that you like. Maybe start by adding a green smoothie bowl to your breakfast routine, we've got a great recipe in PART 2! Then, once you're comfortable with that, try going vegan fur lunch. Make our delicious pasta salad with chickpeas or pick up some Asian takeout (pro tip: Asian restaurants have many dishes that are naturally vegan). Keep slowly adding the vegan foods that you like and watch in amazement as you no longer crave that hamburger or pass on that pizza.

Avoid These Common Mistakes

You are going to make mistakes on your vegan journey. Everyone does, that's how you learn! However, there are some common slip-ups that can be avoided, read on for my advice.

1. Being unprepared – Got a 6-hour flight coming up? You don't want to be on a flight with no vegan option, believe me, it's not fun. Check with your airline to see if they offer a vegan meal. If not, pack a sandwich (we recommend tofu and avocado or a PB&J) then research the first place that you can buy vegan food once you get off of your plane. You'll also want to be prepared when going out to eat. Make sure you check out the menu before you arrive at the restaurant. You may need to eat something light before you go if the only option is a salad.

Make sure you call the restaurant and ask the chef if they have a vegan option that is not listed on the menu, you'll be surprised at how many do!

2. Not being open and honest about your diet choices – Once you're at the restaurant, tell your server that you are vegan. Don't be shy, you're paying for your meal! Make sure that they understand what it means (many servers don't know) and ask what options on the menu are suitable for you.

3. Excuses – "It's too hard, I'm not a good cook, they had free pizza at work," excuses, excuses, excuses. Don't fall for the trap, it's a slippery slope. Stay firm to your commitment!

4. Loading up on carbs – this is a common one. Most new vegans remove the meat from a dish and then add more carbs to make the dish filling. For instance, a rookie vegan might make half a package of pasta with just pasta sauce on top. That's a no-no, unless you're looking to gain weight. Because you will! Instead of removing your protein, replace it with a plant-based protein like beans, tofu, or mock meat.

5. Skipping on protein – this is important! You will likely not feel full and satisfied if you're not getting enough protein. In every meal you should be thinking about where your protein is coming from. Some other great sources are nuts, grains, and leafy greens.

Make sure to follow these tips and tricks as you transition to a vegan lifestyle. Also, seek out resources. Join the vegetarian society in your city, watch tons of YouTube videos, search for vegan meetups in your area, follow Instagram and Pinterest pages for inspiration. Seek out new and interesting foods and find a buddy to go with to experience it. If no one that you know is interested in veganism, join a Facebook group and post pictures of your meal there. The recipes in this book are designed to be easy and fun. Make them often, make them for your friends, experiment with them by changing up the ingredients and quantities. This is your opportunity to do something great for yourself and I am so glad that you chose this book to help you along your journey. Which recipe will you try first?

PART II: 100 Foolproof Vegan Recipes

Breakfast

1. Breakfast Burritos
(Prep Time: 10 MIN │ Total Time: 5 MIN │Servings: 6)

Breakfast Burritos are an easy and portable vegan breakfast. Make a batch ahead of time to enjoy throughout the week. The beans are a tasty source of protein and are delicious paired with avocado, lettuce, and tomato.

Ingredients:
- 2 (15 oz) cans Black Beans, drained and rinsed
- ½ cup Vegetable Stock
- 1 tsp Cumin
- 1 tsp Oregano

- 1 tbsp Garlic Powder
- 1 tbsp Onion Powder
- 6 Whole Wheat Tortillas
- 6 – 12 leaves Romaine Lettuce
- 2 Tomatoes, sliced
- 2 Avocados, pit and skin removed, sliced
- 1 ½ cups Salsa

Directions:
1. Place the beans in a medium sized pot over medium heat. Add the vegetable stock, cumin, oregano, garlic powder, and onion powder. Simmer for about 10 minutes.
2. Lay out a whole wheat tortilla and place one or two leaves of romaine lettuce on top followed by a few slices of tomatoes and avocado.
3. Pour the cooked black beans over top and then add about 1 tbsp of salsa. Roll the tortilla into a burrito shape. Repeat until all tortillas have been used and then serve.

2. Banana and Rolled Oats Pancakes
(Prep Time: 10 MIN │Total Time: 30 MIN │Servings: 4)

These pancakes are easy and inexpensive to make. The recipe calls for a blender but if you don't have one, simply substitute the rolled oats with oat flour if available or all-purpose flour instead.

Ingredients:
- 2 cups Rolled Oats
- 2 ripe Bananas
- 1 cup Unsweetened Plant Milk
- 2 tbsp Vegetable Oil or Vegan Butter

Directions:
1. Add the oats, bananas, and plant milk to a blender then process on high until smooth.

2. Heat a large skillet over medium-low heat then add a dab of vegan butter or vegetable oil (just enough to lightly coat the bottom of the pan).
3. Pour about ¼ cup of pancake mix into the skillet and cook until bubbles start to form and pop across the surface, about 2-3 minutes. Flip and cook on the over side for another 2 -3 minutes.
4. Add a little more oil or butter and repeat step 2 until all batter has been used. Serve with fresh fruit and maple syrup.

3. Choco Banana Overnight Oats
(Prep Time: 15 MIN │ Total Time: 15 MIN │ Servings: 4)

This is a delicious recipe for an on the go breakfast. Perfect for lunch or school, your taste buds will be satisfied and your morning hunger will be fulfilled. If you are gluten free, try replacing the oats with buckwheat groats!

Ingredients:
- 2 tbsp Maple Syrup
- 2 tbsp Cacao Powder
- 4 cups Unsweetened Plant Milk
- 2 Bananas, peeled and sliced into rounds
- 2 cups Rolled Oats

- ¼ cup Cacao Nibs

Directions:
1. In a large mixing bowl, whisk together the maple syrup and cacao powder. Once well combined, whisk in the plant milk.
2. Prepare 4 mason jars or portable containers with lids, place a few slices of banana at the bottom of each jar and then fill to about ¾ of the way full with rolled oats, top with more banana slices and cacao nibs.
3. Pour the plant milk mixture over the oats in each jar and then seal with the lid. Place the oats into the refrigerator overnight. Remove from the refrigerator the next day and serve.

4. Breakfast Potato Stir Fry
(Prep Time: 20 MIN │ Total Time: 35 MIN │ Servings: 6)

Peppers, onions, kale, and potatoes blend together with herbs and spices for a hearty and filling breakfast. A great option for large families or as a tasty dish for brunch.

Ingredients:
- 2 tbsp Vegetable Oil
- 6 large Red Potatoes, medium diced
- 1 small Red Onion, medium diced
- 1 Green Bell Pepper, medium diced
- 2 Red Bell Peppers, medium diced
- 4 cups Kale, rough chopped
- 1 tsp Paprika
- ¼ tsp Red Pepper Flakes
- 1 tsp Garlic Powder
- 1 tsp Dried Oregano
- 1 tsp Dried Thyme
- ¼ cup Water

- Salt and Pepper to taste

Directions:
1. Heat the oil in a large skillet over medium heat then add the red potatoes.   Stir fry for about 5-7 minutes or until browned.
2. Place the onion and bell peppers into the skillet and sauté for 4 minutes.
3. Stir in the remaining ingredients and then cover the skillet with a lid, aluminum foil, or parchment paper. Turn the heat to low and cook for 5 minutes.
4. Remove the lid/cover, adjust the seasonings, and serve hot.

5. Turmeric Tofu Scramble
(Prep Time: 10 MIN │Total Time: 25 MIN │Servings: 4)

Spinach and tofu make a perfect flavor combination with savory turmeric and fresh garlic and onions. The simplicity and delicious flavor of this dish make it a classic recipe amongst the vegan community.

Ingredients:
- 1 tbsp Vegetable Oil
- 2 blocks Extra Firm Tofu, drained and pressed
- 2 cups Red Bell Pepper, seeded and chopped
- 1 cup Onion, chopped
- 4 cups Spinach, chopped
- 1 clove Garlic, minced
- 2 tbsp Turmeric Powder
- 1 tbsp Dried Oregano
- Salt and Pepper to taste

Directions:

1. In a large non-stick skillet over medium heat, warm the oil. With your hands, crumble the tofu into small to medium sized chunks and then add to the skillet. Sauté for 5 minutes.
2. Add the bell peppers and onions, sauté for another 3 minutes. Place the spinach into the skillet along with the garlic, turmeric, oregano, salt, and pepper. Stir well to fully incorporate the seasonings. Cook for 2 more minutes and then serve hot.

6. Vegan French Toast
(Prep Time: 10 MIN │Total Time: 25 MIN │Servings: 4)

You can't even tell its vegan! Get ready to be impressed, this French Toast has crisp chewy edges and a tender gooey center. Try it topped with maple syrup and fresh fruit for an extra special treat.

Ingredients:
- 1 fresh French Loaf
- 4 tbsp ground Flax Seeds
- 2 tbsp Water
- 2 cups Unsweetened Plant Milk
- 2 tsp Cinnamon
- ½ tsp Nutmeg
- 2 tbsp Maple Syrup
- ½ tsp Vanilla
- 3 tbsp Vegan Butter

Directions:

1. Cut the French loaf into 6 roughly ¾ inch slices then set aside.
2. In a small bowl whisk together the ground flax seeds and water then rest for 2 minutes to form a "flax egg."
3. In a large bowl whisk together the milk, cinnamon, nutmeg, maple syrup and vanilla. After the flax egg has formed, whisk it into the mixture. Allow the mixture to sit for another 3 minutes.
4. In a large skillet, melt about 1 tsp of vegan butter, then dip a slice of French loaf into the flax and milk mixture to coat well.   Place the soaked bread into the skillet and cook for about 2-3 minutes on each side. Repeat until all of the bread has been cooked.
5. Serve with fresh fruit and maple syrup.

7. Morning Glory Smoothie Bowl
(Prep Time: 10 MIN │Total Time: 20 MIN │Servings: 2)

Smoothie bowls are an excellent way to increase your fruit and vegetable intake. They are also a fun and quick breakfast that is versatile too! The ingredients within this smoothie as well as the toppings can be switched up based on what you have in the fridge or even your mood for the day.

Ingredients:
- 1 frozen Avocado, peeled, cored and rough chopped
- 2 ripe frozen Bananas
- 1 cup Baby Spinach
- 4 Dates, pitted
- ¼ cup Goji Berries, chopped
- ¼ cup Coconut Flakes
- 2 tbsp Chia seeds
- 1 fresh Banana, peeled and sliced
- ¼ cup Toasted Almonds
- 2 tbsp Cacao Nibs

Directions:

1. Place the frozen avocado, frozen banana, spinach, and dates into a high speed blender or food processor. Blend on high until smooth. The mixture should be thick. Avoid blending for too long, the mixture will start to melt.

2. Pour the smoothie evenly into two serving bowls and top with goji berries, coconut flakes, chia seeds, banana slices, toasted almonds and cacao nibs then serve cold.

8. Avocado Toast with Sautéed Mushrooms
(Prep Time: 10 MIN │ Total Time: 20 MIN │ Servings: 4)

Classic avocado toast with an umami twist. This popular savory breakfast is fast, easy, and so delicious. The crunchy toast combined with the creamy avocado and earthy mushrooms is a heavenly combination.

Ingredients:
- 8 slices rustic Sourdough Bread, toasted
- 4 avocados, peeled, pitted, and sliced into strips
- 1 tbsp Vegetable Oil
- 2 cups Cremona Mushrooms, thinly sliced
- ½ tsp Dried Thyme
- ½ tsp Dried Oregano
- Salt and Pepper to taste

Directions:

1. Place the toast onto a serving platter then top with slices of avocado, set aside.
2. Heat the oil in a large skillet over medium heat. Add the mushrooms and sauté for 3 minutes. Season with thyme, oregano, salt and pepper. Cook for 1 more minute and then turn off the heat.
3. Returning to the avocado toast, lightly mash the avocado on the toast and then place about 1 to 2 tbsp mushrooms on each slice. Garish with a bit of salt and pepper then serve.

9. Gluten Free Oatmeal
(Prep Time: 10 MIN │Total Time: 25 MIN │Servings: 2)

There is nothing like a warm bowl of hearty oatmeal to wake you up on a chilly morning! Try this gluten free version made with delicious quinoa and buckwheat.

Ingredients:
- 1 ripe Banana
- ½ tsp Cinnamon
- ½ cup Buckwheat Groats
- ½ cup Quinoa
- 2 cups Water
- 1 cup Unsweetened Plant Milk
- 2 tbsp Maple Syrup
- 1 cup Raspberries
- ½ cup Toasted Almonds or Cashews
- ½ cup Raisins

Directions:

1. Break the banana into pieces and place it into a small bowl with the cinnamon. Mash the banana and cinnamon well.
2. Pour the buckwheat groats, quinoa and water into a medium sized pot over medium heat. Bring to a boil and then reduce to a simmer. Cook for about 10 -12 minutes.
3. Turn the heat to low and then add the plant milk, mashed banana mixture, and maple syrup. Stir to combine well. You can add more or less milk depending on the consistency that you like your oatmeal. Cook for 1 to 2 more minutes until the mixture is creamy.
4. Transfer the oatmeal to serving bowls, top with raspberries, almonds, and raisins then serve.

10. Kale and Tomato Breakfast Polenta Bowl
(Prep Time: 15 MIN │Total Time: 25 MIN │Servings: 4)

Creamy polenta is topped with savory sautéed kale and tomatoes flavored with garlic and oregano. Make this recipe for your next house guests, they'll be raving about your culinary skills!

Ingredients:
- 4 cups Water
- 1 tsp Sea Salt
- 1 cup Polenta
- 1 tbsp Vegetable Oil
- 2 cups Kale, rough chopped
- 3 Roma Tomatoes, rough chopped
- 1 clove Garlic, minced
- ¼ cup Vegetable Stock
- 1 tsp Dried Oregano
- Salt and Pepper to taste
- 2 tbsp Vegan Butter
- ½ cup Vegan Parmesan Cheese

Directions:
1. In a large pot, bring the water and salt to a boil. Once boiling, slowly whisk in the polenta. Continue to stir ensuring that there are no lumps. Reduce the heat to low and simmer for 5 minutes or until the polenta thickens a bit. Cover with a lid and cook for 30 more minutes. Whisk the polenta every few minutes to prevent sticking.
2. Meanwhile, in a large skillet, heat the oil over medium heat and then stir fry the kale for 3 minutes. Add the tomatoes, garlic, vegetable sock and oregano. Season with salt and pepper then reduce the heat to low and simmer for 5 more minutes.

3. Once the polenta is done cooking, turn off the heat then stir in the butter and parmesan cheese. Season with salt and pepper and distribute the polenta evenly amongst 4 serving bowls. Top each bowl with the kale and tomato mixture and then serve.

11. Fruit and Granola Wraps
(Prep Time: 10 MIN │Total Time: 15 MIN │Servings: 4)

These are fun and delicious wraps with a sweet twist. You can try them with any fruit and spread that you like, roll them up and take them as a portable and tasty breakfast.

Ingredients:

- 8 small Whole Wheat Wraps
- ½ cup Almond Butter
- 2 cups Granola
- 1 Banana, peeled and sliced
- 1 cup Strawberries, sliced
- 1 Apple, cored and sliced

Directions:

1. Lay out the whole wheat wraps on a flat surface. Spread each wrap with a tablespoon or two of almond butter then place ¼ cup of granola on top.
2. Add bananas, strawberries, and apples to each wrap in any variation that you like. My favorite combo is strawberry-banana!
3. Once the wraps are filled, simply roll them up from one end to the other and then serve.

12. Peach and Pecan Baked Oatmeal
(Prep Time: 10 MIN │Total Time: 40 MIN │Servings: 6)

This recipe will remind you of a delicious peach cobbler. You'll love the aroma in the kitchen as the dish bakes and the peaches become caramelized. Serve with a side of vegan yogurt.

Ingredients:
- 2 tbsp Ground Flax Seeds
- ¼ cup Water
- 2 cups Rolled Oats
- 1 lb frozen Peaches, peeled and pitted
- ½ cup Pecan pieces
- 2 tsp Cinnamon
- ½ tsp Nutmeg
- 1 tsp Baking Powder
- ¼ tsp Sea Salt
- ¼ cup Maple Syrup
- 1 ½ tsp Vanilla Extract
- 1 ½ cups Unsweetened Plant Milk

Directions:
1. Preheat the oven to 375° F and coat a 9X9 inch baking dish with non-stick spray.
2. In a small bowl, whisk together the ground flax seeds and the water to make a flax egg. Set aside
3. In a large mixing bowl, combine the remaining ingredients except for the plant milk. Using a wooden spoon, stir the mixture to thoroughly combine.
4. Transfer the peach and oat mixture to the prepared baking dish. Pour the plant milk over the mixture and then place the dish into the oven. Bake for 35-40 minutes or until golden brown.

5. Remove the baked oatmeal from the oven and allow to cool for 10 minutes before serving.

13. Pineapple Green Smoothie
(Prep Time: 5 MIN | Total Time: 15 MIN | Servings: 2)

Fruit smoothies are delicious but sometimes are not as filling as one might hope. The serving of quinoa in this recipe is packed with protein which makes you feel satiated after a meal. So try this recipe next time you are craving a sweet, delicious, and filling treat.

Ingredients:
- ½ cup Unsweetened Plant Milk
- ½ cup Pineapple chunks
- 4 cups Baby Spinach
- ¼ cup Ice
- 1 cup Quinoa, cooked and cooled

Directions:
1. Place all of the ingredients into a high speed blender. Process on high until smooth. Serve cold in tall drinking glasses.

14. TLT
(Prep Time: 10 MIN │ Total Time: 25 MIN │ Servings: 4)

You've heard of a BLT, now try a TLT! To make this famous sandwich vegan we replaced the bacon with Tempeh Bacon which can be found at major grocery stores near the tofu.

Ingredients:
- 1 tbsp Vegetable Oil
- 8 oz Tempeh Bacon slices (Try Tofurkey, Lightlife or Sweet Earth)
- 8 slices Whole Wheat Bread, toasted
- 4 slices Tomato
- 4 leaves Lettuce
- 4 tbsp Vegan Mayonnaise

Directions:
1. Heat the oil in a large skillet over medium heat. Place the tempeh in the skillet and cook for 2 to 3 minutes on each side. Remove from the skillet and drain on a paper towel.

2. To assemble the TLT, slather two slices of bread with ½ tbsp of vegan mayonnaise on each side. Layer with tempeh, then tomato and lettuce. Slice in half, diagonally and then serve.

15. Walnut and Chocolate Chip Banana Bread
(Prep Time: 15 MIN │ Total Time: 75 MIN │ Servings: 8)

This banana bread is an extra sweet take on an old classic. Crunchy walnuts and velvety smooth chocolate chips are a delectable accompaniment to this sweet and deliciously dense bread.

Ingredients:
- 2 tbsp Ground Flax Seeds
- 4 tbsp Water
- 3 very ripe Bananas, peeled
- 1/3 cup Vegan Butter, melted
- 1 tsp Baking Soda
- ¼ tsp Sea Salt
- ½ cup Maple Syrup
- 1 tsp Vanilla Extract
- 1 ½ cups All-Purpose Flour
- ½ cup Vegan Chocolate Chips
- ½ cup Walnuts, chopped

Directions:
1. Preheat the oven to 350° F and coat a 4x8-inch loaf pan with non-stick spray.

2. In a small bowl, whisk together the flax seeds and water to create a flax egg. Set aside.
3. In a large mixing bowl, mash the bananas with a fork until completely smooth then add in the melted butter, stir well to fully incorporate.
4. Next add the baking soda and salt followed by the maple syrup, flax egg, and vanilla extract. Once well combined stir in the flour, chocolate chips, and walnuts.
5. Pour the batter into the prepared loaf pan. Bake for 50 minutes to 1 hour or until a toothpick inserted into the middle comes out clean.
6. Remove the loaf from the oven and cool in the pan for about 5 minutes before slicing and serving.

16. Apple and Sweet Potato Hash Browns
(Prep Time: 15 MIN │Total Time: 40 MIN │Servings: 4)

These hash browns are a nice mix of sweet and savory. Make them ahead of time and carry them to work or school with you! They taste great with vegan Greek yogurt or serve them as a side dish at your next vegan brunch!

Ingredients:
- 2 large Sweet Potatoes
- 2 Green Apples
- 1tbsp + 3 tbsp Vegetable Oil
- ¼ cup All-Purpose or Gluten Free Flour
- ¼ tsp Cinnamon
- Dash Allspice
- ¼ tsp Sea Salt
- ¼ tsp Black Pepper

Directions:
1. Peel the sweet potatoes and apples, then finely shred them on a box shredder. Place the shreds into a large mixing bowl and add 1 tbsp

vegetable oil, flour, cinnamon, allspice, sea salt, and black pepper. Stir well to combine.

2. Heat the remaining oil in a large skillet over medium heat. Once the oil is hot, shape the apple and sweet potato mixture into thin, round patties. Place the patties into the oil and fry for 2-3 minutes on each side, until golden brown.   Remove the patties from the oil and drain on a piece of paper towel. Do this until all of the mixture has been cooked. Serve the hash browns hot.

17. Avocado and Mushroom English Muffin
(Prep Time: 10 MIN │ Total Time: 25 MIN │ Servings: 4)

In the mood for a breakfast sandwich? Just sear up some portabella mushrooms and breakfast will be ready in a flash. This is a versatile dish so sub the kale for spinach or the portabella for tofu, have it your way!

Ingredients:
- ¼ cup Soy Sauce
- 2 tbsp Water
- 2 tbsp + 1 tbsp Olive Oil
- 1tsp Italian Seasoning
- Salt and Pepper to taste
- 4 large Portabella Mushroom Tops, stems removed
- 4 large leaves of Kale
- 4 slices Vegan Pepper Jack Cheese (or any other sliced vegan cheese available).
- 1 Avocado, peeled, pitted, and sliced
- ¼ cup Vegan Mayonnaise
- 2 tbsp Dijon Mustard
- 4 English Muffins, sliced in half and toasted

Directions:

1. In a large bowl, whisk together the soy sauce, water, 2 tbsp olive oil, Italian seasoning and a pinch of salt and pepper. With a fork, poke holes in the mushrooms and then toss them in the soy sauce mixture. Allow the mushrooms to marinate while you proceed with the rest of the recipe.
2. Heat the remaining tbsp of olive oil in a large skillet over medium heat, then add the whole kale leaves and sauté for 2 minutes. Season with salt and pepper and then remove from the skillet and reserve for later.
3. Remove the mushrooms from the marinade and place them into the same skillet, top side down. Reduce the heat to low and sear the mushrooms for 3 minutes then flip. Pour the remaining marinade over the mushrooms and cook for another 3 minutes until tender.
4. After the mushrooms are tender, while still in the skillet, place a kale leaf on top of each mushroom and then layer over a slice of vegan cheese. Cook for about 2 more minutes or until the cheese is melted.
5. In a small bowl, whisk together the mayonnaise and Dijon mustard. Assemble the sandwiches by slathering each side of the bun with a bit of the mayo-dijon sauce then top with the mushrooms and kale, ending with a few slices of avocado and the top of the muffin. Serve hot.

18. Chickpea Toast

(Prep Time: 5 MIN │Total Time: 20 MIN │Servings: 4)

If you are looking for an alternative to avocado toast, here it is! This flavorful and filling breakfast is packed with fiber and is ready in no time.

Ingredients:
- 1 tbsp Vegetable Oil
- 1 (15 oz) can Chickpeas, drained and rinsed
- 1 (8 oz) jar Pizza Sauce
- 8 slices Sour Dough Bread, toasted
- 1 cup Vegan Mozzarella Cheese Shreds
- 1 tbsp Olive Oil
- 1 tbsp Italian Seasoning

Directions:
1. Heat the vegetable oil in a medium sized skillet over medium heat. Add the chickpeas and sauté for about 2 – 3 minutes then add the pizza sauce and reduce the heat to low. Simmer the chickpeas in the pizza sauce for 3 minutes then turn off the heat.
2. To assemble, place two slices of toasted bread on a serving plate. Top each slice with a few scoops of chickpeas then garnish with a pinch of mozzarella cheese, a drizzle of olive oil, and few sprinkles of Italian seasoning. Repeat this with the remaining toast and then serve.

19. Spicy Jalapeno Bagel Sandwich
(Prep Time: 10 MIN | Total Time: 20 MIN | Servings: 4)

Don't miss out on this delicious and savory bagel sandwich. It's refreshing and creamy with just the right amount of spice to wake you up in the morning!

Ingredients:

- 1 cup Vegan Plain Cream Cheese (Kite Hill, Daiya, Follow Your Heart, and Tofutti are all good!)
- 1 tsp fresh Lime Juice
- 1 Jalapeno, finely chopped
- Salt and Pepper to taste
- 4 Whole Wheat Bagels, sliced and toasted
- 1 Cucumber, Sliced into rounds
- 4 slices Tomato
- 1 cup Arugula (also known as Rocket)

Directions:

1. In a medium sized bowl, use a fork to mix together the cream cheese, lime juice, jalapeno, salt, and pepper.
2. To assemble the sandwiches, slather each side of a bagel with the cream cheese mixture then top one side with cucumber, tomato,

and arugula. Place the other side of the bagel on top. Repeat this until all of the bagels are used and then serve.

20. Fruit and Cashew Ricotta Toast
(Prep Time: 15 MIN │Total Time: 25 MIN │Servings: 6)

This is an easy recipe to make gluten free. Just replace the whole wheat bread with your favorite gluten free bread.   Make sure you read the label! Some gluten free breads contain eggs or dairy!

Ingredients:
- 1 ½ cups Cashews, soaked overnight
- ¼ cup Water
- 1 tbsp fresh Lemon Juice
- Pinch Sea Salt
- 12 slices Whole Wheat Bread, toasted
- 1 cup Blueberries
- 1 Peach, pitted and thinly sliced
- 2 tbsp Maple Syrup

Directions:
1. Place the cashews, water, lemon juice, and sea salt in a food processor. Blend on high until the mixture reaches a smooth yet grainy consistency, about 2 minutes.
2. Slather each slice of toasted bread with the cashew ricotta then generously top with the blueberries and peaches. Drizzle each slice with maple syrup and serve.

Soup and Stew

21. Tomato Basil Soup
(Prep Time: 25 MIN │Total Time: 50 MIN │Servings: 4)

This soup makes a delicious lunch or a great salad accompaniment for dinner. It's satisfying without being too heavy so you can make this recipe all year-round. For a little crunch, try it topped with croutons or sunflower seeds.

Ingredients:

- 3 lbs Tomatoes, sliced in half
- 1 Onion, quartered
- 4 cloves Garlic
- 2 tbsp Olive Oil
- Salt and Pepper to taste
- 1 cup Vegetable stock

- ½ cup Unsweetened Plant Milk
- ½ cup Basil Leaves, sliced chiffonade (reserve some for garnish)

Directions:
1. Preheat the oven to 375º F then line a baking sheet with parchment paper.
2. Add the tomatoes, onion, garlic, and olive oil to a large bowl. Season with salt and pepper then toss well. Arrange the tomato mixture onto the baking sheet and then place it into the oven to roast for 10 minutes.
3. Take the baking sheet out of the oven, transfer the garlic to a blender and then place the baking sheet back into the oven for 15 more minutes.
4. Once the tomatoes have roasted, add them into the blender with the garlic and pour in the vegetable stock. Blend on high for about 3 minutes or until the mixture is smooth.
5. Transfer the soup into a large pot over low heat and bring it to a simmer. Add the plant milk and heat for another 5 minutes. Stir in the basil, and season to taste with salt and pepper.
6. Serve in soup bowls garnished with basil.

22. Lentil Stew
(Prep Time: 10 MIN │Total Time: 30 MIN │Servings: 4)

Here is a simple and delicious recipe to make after work or whenever there is limited time to prepare dinner. Using prepared foods in recipes is a great way to make your vegan journey a little bit easier.

Ingredients:
- 1 lb Frozen Mixed Vegetables
- 1 cup Dried Barley
- 2 Red Potatoes, medium diced
- 2 Roma Tomatoes, medium diced
- 1 cup Dried Lentils, washed and rinsed
- 4 cups Kale
- 4 cups Vegetable Stock
- Salt and Pepper to taste

Directions:
1. In a large pot over medium-low heat, add the frozen vegetables, barley, potatoes, tomatoes, lentils, and vegetable stock. Season with salt and pepper then simmer for 20 minutes.
2. Stir in the kale, simmer for 10 more minutes and then serve hot.

23. Spinach and White Bean Soup with Orecchiette
(Prep Time: 10 MIN │ Total Time: 35 MIN │ Servings: 6)

Make this recipe for a girl's night in or a pot luck at the office. It's great for many occasions! Your guests will love the flavorful broth and creamy white beans. They'll never know that it was so simple to make!

Ingredients:

- 8 oz dried Orecchiette pasta
- 1 tbsp Vegetable Oil
- 1 ½ cups Onion, small diced
- 1 cup Carrots, small diced
- 1 cup Celery, small diced
- 2 cloves Garlic, finely chopped
- 1 (15 oz) can Cannellini, drained and rinsed
- 3 cups Vegetable Stock
- ½ tsp fresh Thyme
- ½ tsp fresh Oregano
- Salt and Pepper to taste
- 2 lbs Baby Spinach

Directions:

1. Cook the orecchiette according to package instructions and then set aside.
2. Heat the vegetable oil in a large pot over medium-low heat. Sautee the onion, carrots, and celery until tender, about 5 minutes. Add the garlic and sauté for 3 more minutes.
3. Add the beans, thyme, oregano, salt, pepper, and vegetable stock. Simmer on low for 20 minutes. Stir in the spinach and orecchiette then cook for 5 more minutes. Serve hot in a soup bowl.

24. Butternut Squash Vegan Chili
(Prep Time: 10 MIN | Total Time: 50 MIN | Servings: 6)

Classic chili just got a sweet twist. This is a delicious and warming recipe that is perfect for the colder months. Plus, it's versatile! Try it on top of french fries or on top of a vegan burger with vegan cheese.

Ingredients:
- 1 tbsp Vegetable Oil
- 1 cup Onion, diced
- 1 medium Butternut Squash, peeled, seeded, and medium diced
- 3 tbsp Chili Powder
- 1 tbsp Cumin
- ½ tsp Red Pepper Flakes
- 2 cloves Garlic, minced
- 1 (15 oz) can Red Kidney Beans, drained and rinsed
- 1 (15 oz) can Black Beans, drained and rinsed
- 2 Tomatoes, diced
- ¼ cup Tomato Paste
- 2 cups Vegetable Stock
- Salt and Pepper to taste

Directions:
1. Heat the vegetable oil in a large pot over medium heat. Add the onions and sauté for 3 minutes.
2. Place the butternut squash into the pot and sauté for about 7 minutes. Stir in the chili powder, cumin, red pepper flakes, and garlic then sauté for another 2 minutes.
3. Pour in the red kidney beans, black beans, tomatoes and tomato paste. Add the vegetable stock and season with salt and pepper.
4. Simmer for 25 minutes or until the butternut squash is tender and the stew has thickened. Serve hot with cornbread or crackers.

25. Tangy Turmeric Roasted Cauliflower Soup
(Prep Time: 10 MIN │ Total Time: 40 MIN │ Servings: 4)

A tasty and warming soup with all the health benefits of turmeric. A bit of lemon juice is added for a touch of tang to balance out the earthy spices. Enjoy this soup for lunch or dinner!

Ingredients:
- 2 heads Cauliflower, chopped into 1 inch pieces
- 2 tbsp Vegetable Oil
- 1 small White Onion, sliced into quarters
- 3 tbsp Turmeric Powder
- 1 tsp Cumin Powder
- 3 cloves Garlic
- 4 cups Vegetable Stock
- 1 Lemon, juiced
- Salt and Pepper to taste

Directions:
1. Preheat the oven to 375° F and line a baking sheet with parchment paper.
2. In a large mixing bowl, toss together the cauliflower, oil, turmeric, and cumin. Arrange the contents of the mixing bowl onto the prepared baking sheet in one layer. Place the baking sheet into the oven for 25 minutes. Stir once halfway through.
3. Once the cauliflower is tender, remove the sheet tray from the oven and place the contents into a high speed blender along with the garlic and about a cup of vegetable stock. Process on high until smooth.
4. Pour the soup into a large pot over medium-low heat. Add the remaining vegetable stock, lemon juice, and then season with salt and pepper. Simmer for about 2 minutes and then serve.

26. Spiced Creamy Coconut Vegetable Soup
(Prep Time: 10 MIN │Total Time: 35 MIN │Servings: 4)

Creamy coconut milk enhances the flavor and texture of this delectably spiced soup. Try it with a side of naan or pita bread for a delicious dipping sensation.

Ingredients:
- 2 tbsp Vegetable Oil
- 2 Sweet Potatoes, peeled and medium diced
- 3 Bell Peppers (any color) seeded and medium diced
- 2 cups Onion, medium diced
- 1 tbsp Paprika
- Pinch Red Pepper Flakes
- 2 cloves Garlic, minced
- 1 (14 oz) can Coconut Milk
- 1 Lime, juiced
- 4 cups Kale, rough chopped
- 1 bunch Cilantro, chopped
- Salt and Pepper to taste

Directions:
1. Heat the oil in a large pot over medium heat then sauté the sweet potatoes for 3 minutes.
2. Add the bell peppers, onions, paprika, red pepper flakes, and garlic. Sauté for an additional 2 minutes. Pour in the coconut milk and lime juice then reduce the heat and simmer for about 15 minutes.
3. Place the kale and cilantro into the pot and then season with salt and pepper. Cook for 5 additional minutes then serve hot.

27. Vegan Taco Soup
(Prep Time: 5 MIN │Total Time: 30 MIN │Servings: 4)

A perfect party dish! You can play with the spice in this recipe by either omitting the jalapeno or adding more. This soup doubles as a dip, try it with your favorite tortilla chips.

Ingredients:
- 1 tbsp Vegetable Oil
- 1 cup Onion, diced
- 2 cloves Garlic, minced
- 1 (15 oz) can Black Beans, drained and rinsed
- 1 (15 oz) can Whole Kernel Corn, drained
- 1 cup dried Lentils
- 1 package Taco Seasoning
- 1 (15 oz) can Crushed Tomatoes
- 1 cup Tomato Sauce (Tomato Puree)
- 2 cups Vegetable Stock
- Tortilla Chips (optional for dipping)

Directions:
1. Heat the oil in a large pot over low heat. Sauté the onion and garlic for 3 minutes. Add the remaining ingredients into the pot. Turn the heat to medium and simmer for 20 minutes.
2. Once the lentils are tender, turn off the heat and serve with a side of tortilla chips.

28. Creamy Black Bean Soup
(Prep Time: 10 MIN │ Total Time: 50 │ Servings: 6)

You'll love this delicious and filling soup. If you've ever heard that vegans are always hungry, this soup with prove that fake news wrong! Try it with avocado and a scoop of vegan sour cream on top!

Ingredients:
- 2 tbsp Vegetable Oil
- 1 Onion, rough chopped
- 1 large Carrot, peeled and rough chopped
- 3 Celery Ribs, rough chopped
- 6 cloves Garlic, rough chopped
- 4 (15-ounce) cans Black Beans, drained and rinsed
- 1 Jalapeno, rough chopped
- 1 ½ tbsp Ground Cumin
- 4 cups Vegetable Stock
- 1 Lime, juiced
- Salt and Pepper to taste

Directions:
1. Heat the oil in a large pot over low heat. Sauté the onion, carrot, celery, and garlic for 3 minutes.
2. Add the remaining ingredients and bring to a simmer. Cook for 15 minutes. If you have an immersion blender, submerge the stick into the soup and blend until creamy. Otherwise, in small batches, carefully pour the contents into a blender and blend until smooth. Return the soup to the pot and reheat on low for 3 minutes.

29. Cream of Broccoli Soup
(Prep Time: 15 MIN │ Total Time: 35 MIN │ Servings: 6)

This one's for the broccoli lover in you! If you don't have time to soak the cashews overnight, boil some water and pour over the cashews and soak for 30 minutes. Your delicious soup will be just as creamy!

Ingredients:
- 1 tbsp Vegetable Oil
- 1 medium Onion, rough chopped
- 2 Carrots, rough chopped
- 2 stalks Celery, rough chopped
- 3 cloves Garlic, minced
- 2 heads Broccoli, rough chopped
- 6 cups Vegetable Stock
- 1 cup Cashews, soaked overnight
- Salt and Pepper to taste

Directions:

1. Heat the oil in a large pot over medium heat. Sauté the onion, carrots, and celery for 3 minutes. Next add the garlic and broccoli and sauté for 3 minutes more.

2. Pour in the vegetable stock and cashews then season with salt and pepper. Bring to a simmer and cook for 5 minutes. Once the broccoli is tender, add the contents to a blender and process until smooth. Return the soup to the pot and reheat for 3 minutes then serve hot.

30. Chickpea, Arugula, and Mushroom Stew
(Prep Time: 10 MIN | Total Time: 35 MIN | Servings: 4)

This stew is packed with savory, umami flavor. Make it for dinner and then pack some for lunch tomorrow! It's simple, delicious and healthy. Tastes great with a crunchy sourdough bread. Try it tonight!

Ingredients:
- 1 tbsp Vegetable Oil
- 2 cups White Onion, medium diced
- 4 cups Cremini Mushrooms, thickly sliced
- 3 cloves Garlic, chopped
- 1 (15 oz) can Chickpeas, drained and rinsed
- 1 (8 oz) can Diced Tomatoes
- 2 cups Vegetable Stock
- 3 cups Arugula, packed (also known as Rocket)
- Salt and Pepper to taste

Directions:
1. Heat the oil in a large pot over medium heat. Sauté the onion, mushrooms, and garlic for 3 minutes. Once the garlic and onions are fragrant and the mushrooms have shrunken in size, add the chickpeas, tomatoes, and vegetable stock. Bring to a simmer and cook for 15 minutes
2. Add the arugula, season with salt and pepper, and then simmer for 5 more minutes. Serve hot with a nice crunchy bread.

Main Course

31. Pasta Salad with Seared Tofu
(Prep Time: 20 MIN │Total Time: 10 MIN │Servings: 6)

This recipe is incredibly tasty! The tofu is full of protein so you'll be satiated until your next meal. The tangy lemon vinaigrette is a perfect complement to this delicious pasta salad.

Ingredients:
- 1 tsp Vegetable Oil
- 1 block Tofu, drained and pressed
- 3 cups Spinach
- 1 Lemon, zested and juiced
- 1 tbsp Olive Oil
- 1 package Rotini Pasta, cooked
- 1 cup Red Onions, chopped
- 2 cups Cherry Tomatoes, sliced in half
- 1 clove Garlic, minced

- Salt and Pepper to taste

Directions:

1. In a large skillet, heat the vegetable oil over medium heat.
2. Slice the tofu lengthwise into 6 equal sized pieces then sear the tofu for about 10 minutes, flip the tofu half way through. Season with salt and pepper to taste. Once the tofu has browned, remove it from the pan and set aside to cool.
3. To a large mixing bowl, add the spinach, lemon juice, zest, and olive oil then stir.
4. Chop the cooled tofu into medium sized pieces and then add it to the spinach bowl along with the pasta, onions, tomatoes, and garlic to the mixture. Season with salt and pepper then toss well and either serve at room temperature or place in the refrigerator for 2 hours and then serve cold.

32. Asian Quinoa Salad
(Prep Time: 25 MIN │Total Time: 45 MIN │Servings: 4)

A quinoa salad with an Asian zing. Protein rich quinoa is tossed together with crisp vegetables for this Asian inspired dish. Have this for lunch or as a side dish for dinner!

Ingredients:
- 2 cups Quinoa, cooked
- 1 cup Carrots, grated
- 1 cup Red Cabbage, grated
- 1 cup Napa Cabbage, shredded
- 1 cup Red Bell Pepper, julienned
- 1 cup Green Bell Pepper, julienned
- 2 cups Kale, shredded
- 1 ½ cups Almonds, toasted
- ¼ cup Creamy Peanut Butter
- 1 Lime, zested and juiced

- 1 tbsp Sesame Seeds
- 1 tsp Soy Sauce
- 2 tbsp Water

Directions:
1. In a large mixing bowl, toss together the quinoa, carrots, red and Napa cabbage, red and green bell peppers, kale, and almonds.
2. To make the dressing, whisk together the peanut butter, lime zest and juice, sesame seeds, soy sauce, and water in a small bowl.
3. Pour the dressing over the salad and toss to combine well then serve.

33. Red Beans and Rice
(Prep Time: 20 MIN | Total Time: 45 MIN | Servings: 6)

A taste of Cajun flavor right in your own kitchen. This recipe is simple, delicious, and satisfyingly filling. Try it with a slice of homemade cornbread!

Ingredients:
- 1 tbsp Vegetable Oil
- ½ cup Onions, chopped
- ½ cup Carrots, chopped
- ½ cup Celery, chopped
- 3 cloves Garlic, chopped
- 2 (15 oz) cans Red Beans, drained and rinsed
- 2 cups Vegetable Broth
- 2 tbsp Cajun Seasoning
- 2 cups Brown Rice, cooked
- 2 tbsp Vegan Butter
- Salt and Pepper to taste

Directions:
1. Heat the oil in a large pot over low heat, then sauté the onions, carrots, celery, and garlic for 5 minutes.
2. Add the red beans, vegetable broth, and Cajun seasoning to the pot. Turn the heat to medium and bring to a simmer. Allow to cook for 20 minutes.
3. Place the brown rice and vegan butter into the pot with the beans, stir well to combine Season with salt and pepper to taste and then serve.

34. Zoodles in Cashew Alfredo Sauce
(Prep Time: 20 MIN | Total Time: 35 MIN | Servings: 4)

This is the healthiest alfredo pasta you've ever had! It's quick, easy, and delicious. Try this creamy vegan pasta alternative tonight!

Ingredients:
- 2 tbsp Vegetable Oil
- 4 large Zucchinis, grated into noodles
- 2 cups Cashews, soaked overnight
- ½ cup Vegetable Stock
- ¼ cups Unsweetened Plant Milk
- ½ cup Nutritional Yeast
- 4 cloves Garlic, roasted
- ½ cup Onion, rough chopped
- 1 Lemon, juiced
- ½ cup Sun Dried Tomatoes
- Salt and Pepper to taste

Directions:
1. In a large skillet, heat the vegetable oil over medium heat.
2. Sauté the zoodles in the oil for 3 – 4 minutes or until slightly softened.
3. Meanwhile, drain the cashews and add them to a blender along with the vegetable stock, plant milk, nutritional yeast, roasted garlic, onion, and lemon juice. Blend the mixture on high until smooth.
4. Add the alfredo sauce into the pan with the zoodles, then place the sun dried tomatoes into the pan as well, toss to combine. Reduce the heat to low and cook for 2 more minutes. Add more vegetable stock if the sauce is too thick and then serve.

35. Gochujang Lentils with Rice
(Prep Time: 30 MIN │Total Time: 45 MIN │Servings: 4)

Give your lentils some Korean flair with this simple and delicious recipe. Gochujang sauce can be found in the international section at your local grocery store. Try them served with steamed broccoli or sautéed spinach.

Ingredients:
- 1 tbsp Vegetable Oil
- ¼ cup white onion, chopped
- 1 clove Garlic, chopped
- 1 cup Brown Lentils, soaked for 30 mins
- 1 cup Vegetable Stock
- ¼ cup Gochujang Sauce
- 2 cups Brown Rice, cooked
- 1 Lime, juiced
- 2 tbsp Green Onions, chopped

Directions:
1. Heat the oil in a large skillet over low heat. Sauté the onion and garlic for two minutes.
2. Add the lentils and vegetable stock to the skillet and simmer for 15 minutes. Stir in the gochujang sauce.
3. In a bowl, combine the rice, lime juice, and green onions. Toss to mix well.
4. Serve the rice in bowl topped with the flavored lentils.

36. Cajun Chickpea Burgers
(Prep Time: 20 MIN │ Total Time: 20 MIN │ Servings: 4)

Missing burgers? Never fear, chickpea burgers are here! Make these ahead of time and take them as a delicious lunch for work or school. Serve them with a salad of some delicious veggie chips.

Ingredients:
- 1 (15 oz) can Chickpeas, drained and rinsed
- 1 cup Millet, cooked
- 1/2 cup Onion, small diced
- 1 cup Zucchini, grated
- 2 tbsp Cajun Seasoning
- 1 tbsp Cilantro, finely chopped
- 2 tbsp Olive Oil
- 1 Lime, juiced
- 1 clove Garlic, minced
- 1 tsp Cumin Powder
- Salt and Pepper to taste

Directions:
1. In a medium sized bowl, mash the chickpeas and millet then add the onion, zucchini, Cajun seasoning, cilantro, olive oil, lime juice, garlic, cumin powder, salt, pepper, and vegetable oil. Stir the mixture to combine well.
2. Preheat the oven to 400° F then shape 1/3 cup portions into patties. Place the patties onto a baking sheet lined with parchment paper, then add to the hot oven for 20 minutes. Flip the burgers after 10 minutes of cooking.
3. Serve the patties hot with your favorite burger toppings.

37. Coconut Green Curry
(Prep Time: 15 MIN │Total Time: 40 MIN │Servings: 4)

Make this quick green curry when you want a delicious and fulfilling meal prepared I a short amount of time. This is a wonderfully customizable dish, so add any other vegetables that you like!

Ingredients:
- 1 tbsp Vegetable Oil
- 1 block Tofu, drained and pressed
- 2 Bell Peppers (any color), julienned
- ¼ cup Onion
- ¼ cup Green Curry Paste
- 1 (13.5 oz) can Coconut Milk
- 3 cups Spinach

Directions:
1. Heat the oil in a large skillet over medium heat. Chop the tofu into medium sized diced pieces and then sauté the pieces in the hot oil for 5 minutes.
2. Add the bell peppers and onions to the skillet and cook for 3 minutes. Next add the curry paste and then pour in the coconut milk. Allow to simmer for 5 -7 minutes. If the mixture is too thick, add a little water.
3. Stir in the spinach and simmer for 2 more minutes. Serve over rice.

38. Spaghetti and Meat-less Balls
(Prep Time: 15 MIN │Total Time: 35 MIN │Servings: 4)

A meatless version of a classic favorite. Enjoy this quick meal after work or as tasty weekend lunch. Serve with a side salad to stretch it a bit more.

Ingredients:
- 4 servings Whole Wheat Pasta, cooked
- 12 Gardein Meatless Meatballs
- 1 Jar Pasta Sauce

Directions:
1. Cook the pasta according to the package directions. Set aside.
2. Place the meatless balls and the pasta sauce into a large skillet over medium heat. Warm through for about 5 – 7 minutes.
3. Serve the meatless balls in sauce over the pasta.

39. Curried Beans
(Prep Time: 10 MIN │Total Time: 35 MIN │Servings: 4)

A creamy and delicious bean curry that tastes great served with pita, or on top of toast. Feel free to serve it with rice or salad greens for a complete meal.

Ingredients:
- 1 tbsp Vegetable Oil
- ½ tsp Cumin Powder
- ¼ tsp Garam Masala
- ¼ tsp Turmeric
- 1 cup Red Onion, Chopped
- 2 cloves Garlic, chopped
- 1 Green Chili, chopped
- 1 (14 oz) can Diced Tomatoes
- ½ cup Black Beans
- ½ cup Kidney Beans
- ½ cup Navy Beans
- 1 tsp Curry Powder
- ¼ tsp Red Pepper Flakes
- 1 ½ cups Water
- ½ cup Coconut Milk
- Salt and Pepper, to taste
- 2 tbsp Lemon juice
- 2 tbsp Cilantro, chopped

Directions:
1. Heat the oil in a large skillet over medium heat. Cook the cumin, garam masala, and turmeric for 1 minute before adding the onion, garlic, and green chili. Sauté for another 3 minutes.
2. Add in the tomatoes, beans, curry powder, red pepper flakes, water and coconut milk. Simmer the mixture for 10 minutes

3. Season with salt and pepper then stir in lemon juice and cilantro then serve.

40. Stuffed Peppers

(Prep Time: 20 MIN │ Total Time: 45 MIN │ Servings: 6)

A gluten free dish that is healthy and delicious! If you have shredded vegan cheese on hand, feel free to top the peppers with a sprinkle or two.

Ingredients:
- 6 large Red Bell Peppers
- 1 tbsp Vegetable Oil
- 1 cup White Mushrooms, chopped
- 1 cup Onion, chopped
- 1 clove Garlic, chopped
- 1 (15 oz) can Black Beans, drained and rinsed
- 2 cups Brown Rice, cooked
- 1 packet Taco seasoning
- 2 tbsp Water

Directions:
1. Preheat the oven to 375º F and line a baking sheet with parchment paper.
2. Chop the top off of the bell peppers then remove the seeds. Arrange the bell peppers on the baking sheet, cut side up and then set aside.
3. Heat the oil in a large skillet over medium heat. Sauté the mushrooms, onion, and garlic for 3 minutes.
4. Stir in the beans, rice, taco seasoning, and water. Cook for another 2 or 3 minutes then distribute the mixture evenly between the bell peppers.
5. Place the bell peppers into the oven and bake for 15 minutes. Remove peppers from the oven and then serve.

41. Mandarin Sesame Soba Noodles with Edamame
(Prep Time: 15 MIN │Total Time: 25 MIN │Servings: 4)

Hearty and chewy soba noodles paired with a sweet and savory sauce and tossed with crunchy edamame. This is an excellent dish for lunch or dinner!

Ingredients:
- 2 Mandarin Oranges
- 1 tsp Sesame Oil
- 1 Lime, zested and juiced
- Salt and Pepper to taste
- 1 cup Edamame, steamed, shell removed
- 1 package Soba Noodles, cooked
- 1 tbsp Sesame Seeds

Directions:
1. In a large serving bowl, slightly mash the mandarin oranges to release some of the juice. Pour in the sesame oil, lime zest and juice and a dash of salt and pepper.
2. Add in the edamame and soba noodles then toss mix well. Top the noodles with sesame seeds and serve.

42. Mushroom Tacos
(Prep Time: 15 MIN │ Total Time: 35 MIN │ Servings: 4)

Meaty mushrooms are the star of this flavor fiesta! Try these served with a side of black beans and rice.

Ingredients:
- 4 large Portabella Caps
- 1 tbsp Vegetable Oil
- 2 tbsp Taco Seasoning
- 4 Taco Shells
- 1 Avocado, pitted and sliced
- 1 Tomato, chopped
- 2 tbsp Cilantro, chopped
- ¼ cup Red Onion, thinly sliced

Directions:
1. Cut the mushrooms into thin slices then toss them in a medium sized bowl with the oil and taco seasoning.
2. Heat a skillet over medium heat and then sauté the mushrooms for 5 minutes.
3. To serve, top a flour tortilla with avocado, tomato, cilantro and onion.

43. Veggie Fried Rice
(Prep Time: 20 MIN | Total Time: 35 MIN | Servings: 4)

This stir fry is loaded with veggies and healthy brown rice. Use the vegetables suggested in the recipe or whatever you have on hand.

Ingredients:
- 2 tbsp Soy Sauce
- 1 tbsp Water
- 1 tsp Rice Wine Vinegar
- 1 clove Garlic, minced
- 1 tbsp Vegetable Oil
- ¼ cup Carrots, chopped
- ½ cup Snow Peas
- ½ cup Bell Peppers
- ½ cup Button Mushrooms
- ¼ cup Onions
- 1 cup Broccoli Florets
- 1 cup Cauliflower Florets
- ½ cup Peas
- 2 cups Brown Rice, cooked and cooled

Directions:
1. In a small bowl whisk together the soy sauce, water, vinegar, and garlic. Set aside.
2. Heat the oil in a large non-stick skillet over high heat. Quickly sauté the vegetables and then add the rice. Stir fry for 3 more minutes then and the sauce and cook for 2 more minutes. Serve hot.

44. Spinach and Mushroom Sauté
(Prep Time: 10 MIN │Total Time: 25 MIN │Servings: 4)

This recipe is super healthy, tasty, and gluten free! Plus, you'll love the garlicky flavor. Try it served with rice or over your favorite pasta.

Ingredients:
- 1 tbsp Vegetable Oil
- 2 cups Cremini Mushrooms, thinly sliced
- 2 cloves Garlic, minced
- 4 lbs Spinach
- Salt and Pepper to taste

Directions:
1. Heat the oil in a large skillet with a lid over medium heat then sauté the mushrooms for 3 minutes.
2. Add the garlic, sauté for 1 minute and then pack the spinach into the skillet. Place the lid over the skillet and steam for 2 minutes. Season with salt, stir to incorporate, and pepper then serve.

45. Turmeric Roasted Potatoes and Cauliflower
(Prep Time: 10 MIN │ Total Time: 30 MIN │ Servings: 4)

A hearty meal with deliciously flavored potatoes and cauliflower that are roasted to tender perfection. A green salad pairs perfectly with this dish.

Ingredients:
- 1 head Cauliflower, chopped into bite sized pieces
- 4 Russet Potatoes, chopped into bite sized pieces
- 2 tbsp Vegetable Oil
- 2 tbsp Turmeric
- 1/8 tsp Cayenne
- Salt and Pepper to taste

Directions:
1. Preheat the oven to 375° F and line a baking sheet with parchment paper.
2. Toss all of the ingredients together in a mixing bowl then arrange in one layer on the prepared baking sheet.
3. Add the baking sheet to the oven and roast for 20 minutes, stirring once after 10 minutes.

46. Chickpea Mediterranean Bowl
(Prep Time: 10 MIN │ Total Time: 30 MIN │ Servings: 4)

Taste the flavors of the Mediterranean with simple bowl. Classic combinations come together to satisfy your hunger and leave you feeling light and fulfilled. Try this dish with a side of hummus and pita bread!

Ingredients:
- 1 tbsp Vegetable Oil
- 1 (15 oz) can Chickpeas, drained and rinsed
- 1 tsp Paprika
- 1 tsp Dried Oregano
- Salt and Pepper to taste
- 2 heads Romaine Lettuce, chopped
- 1 cup Cucumber, diced
- 1 cup Tomato, diced
- ½ cup Red Onion, thinly sliced
- 2 cups Quinoa Cooked
- 1 Lemon, juiced
- 2 tbsp Olive Oil

Directions:
1. Heat the vegetable oil in a large skillet over medium heat. Sauté the chickpeas for 5 minutes and then add the paprika, oregano, and a pinch of salt and pepper. Continue to cook for 3 more minutes then remove from the heat.
2. In a serving bowl place romaine lettuce on the bottom then place a portion of cucumber, tomato, red onion, and quinoa in sections over the lettuce.
3. Sprinkle lemon juice and olive oil over top and season with a pinch more salt and pepper.

47. Herbed Corn Fritters
(Prep Time: 30 MIN │Total Time: 50 MIN │Servings: 4)

You'll love the creaminess and intense flavor of the delicious corn fritters. They are so easy to make and make a perfect main dish or accompaniment to a larger meal.

Ingredients:
- 1 lb frozen Corn
- 2 tbsp Vegetable Oil
- Salt and Pepper to taste
- 3 cloves Garlic, minced
- 2 tbsp Cilantro, fresh
- 2 tbsp Parsley, fresh
- 1 tbsp Basil, fresh
- 1 small Red Chili, chopped
- ¼ cup Unsweetened Plant Milk
- ¼ cup Chickpea flour

Directions:
1. Preheat the oven to 375° F and line a baking sheet with parchment paper.
2. In a large mixing bowl toss together the corn, vegetable oil, and a pinch of salt and pepper. Arrange the corn onto the baking sheet in a single layer. Place the baking sheet in the oven for 15 minutes, stirring halfway through.
3. Once the corn has roasted, place it into a food processor along with the remaining ingredients and pulse until well combined.
4. Form the mixture into 8 equally sized patties and then place them onto the baking sheet. Place the baking sheet back into the oven for 15 more minutes, flip the fritters half way through. Serve hot.

48. Green Pea Pilaf
(Prep Time: 10 MIN │ Total Time: 35 MIN │ Servings: 4)

Pilafs are an excellent way to pack in a lot of flavor and nutrients! You'll love this Green Pea pilaf with delicious vegetables and chewy brown rice.

Ingredients:
- 2 tbsp Vegetable Oil
- ¼ cup Onion, chopped
- ¼ cup Carrots, chopped
- ¼ cup Celery, chopped
- 2 cloves garlic, chopped
- 1 ½ cups Brown Rice
- 3 cups Vegetable Stock
- 2 cups Peas, frozen
- 1 cup Tomatoes, chopped
- ¼ cup Almonds, toasted

Directions:
1. Heat the oil in a large pot over low heat. Place the onion, carrot, celery, and garlic in the pot and sweat for 3 minutes. Add the brown rice and stir to combine. Continue stirring to toast the rice for about 2 more minutes.
2. Add the brown rice and vegetable stock and bring the mixture to a simmer. Place the lid on the pot and simmer on low for 15 minutes.
3. Remove the lid and add the peas, tomatoes, and almonds. Stir and return the lid to the pot. Cook for 5 more minutes or until the water is absorbed. Turn off the heat and let the pilaf sit covered for 10 minutes before serving.

49. Spicy Yellow Lentils with Cauliflower
(Prep Time: 20 MIN │ Total Time: 45 MIN │ Servings: 4)

These lentils are perfect for a chili day. They are filling enough to be served alone but taste great over rice or with a slice of your favorite bread.

Ingredients:
- 1 tbsp Vegetable Oil
- 1 cup onion, chopped
- 2 cloves garlic, minced
- 1 tbsp Turmeric Powder
- 2 cups Cauliflower Florets
- 1 cup Yellow Lentils, soaked for 20 mins
- ½ cup Vegetable Stock
- 2 sprigs Fresh Thyme

Directions:
1. Heat the oil in a large pot over medium heat then sauté the onion and garlic for 2 minutes. Add the turmeric and cauliflower then sauté for 3 more minutes.
2. Drain the lentils and then place them into the pot with the cauliflower. Add the vegetable stock and thyme then simmer for 20 minutes.   Serve hot.

50. Chickpea Stuffed Eggplant
(Prep Time: 10 MIN │ Total Time: 45 MIN │ Servings: 4)

A filling and delicious Mediterranean themed dish. The flavor of the creamy chickpeas and the earthiness of the eggplant are a delicious combination with the herbs and spices in this recipe.

Ingredients:
- 2 large Eggplants
- 1 tbsp Olive Oil
- 2 cups Chickpeas, cooked
- ¼ cup Kalamata Olives, chopped
- 1 Roma Tomato, chopped
- 1 tbsp fresh Oregano, chopped
- 1 tbsp fresh Parsley, chopped
- 2 tbsp fresh Lemon Juice
- Salt and Pepper to taste

Directions:
1. Preheat the oven to 375° F and line a baking sheet with parchment paper. Slice the eggplant in half, lengthwise, and then score the inner flesh with hash marks. Rub the inner flesh with olive oil and then season with salt and pepper. Place the eggplant flesh side down onto the prepared baking sheet and add to the oven to roast for 25 minutes.
2. In a large mixing bowl, toss together the remaining ingredients. Once the eggplant is done roasting, scoop out the inner flesh leaving the skin intact. Add the flesh to the mixing bowl and combine.
3. Fill the eggplant skins with the contents of the mixing bowl. Place them back into the oven for another 10 – 15 minutes. Serve hot.

51. Chicken Fried Mushrooms
(Prep Time: 20 MIN │Total Time: 40 MIN │Servings: 4)

Who doesn't love all things fried? Well you're going to love these chicken fried mushrooms. They are crunchy on the outside, tender on the inside and full of delicious flavor.

Ingredients:
- 1 cup Vegetable Oil
- 2 lbs Button Mushrooms
- 1 cup Vegan Yogurt
- 1 tsp Lemon Juice
- 1 tbsp Hot Sauce
- Salt and Pepper to taste
- 2 cups All-Purpose Flour
- 1 tsp Garlic Powder
- 1 tsp Onion Powder
- 1 tsp Paprika

Directions:
1. Wipe the mushrooms with a wet paper towel to clean them. Then heat the oil over medium high heat.
2. In a medium sized mixing bowl whisk together the yogurt, lemon juice, and hot sauce. Season with a pinch of salt and pepper.
3. In another medium sized bowl, whisk together the flour, garlic powder, onion powder, and paprika.
4. One by one, dip the mushrooms into the yogurt mixture, then the flour mixture making sure to coat them completely. Place the mushrooms into the oil and fry until golden brown.
5. Remove from the oil and drain on a piece of paper towel. Serve hot.

52. Roasted Veggies and Cous Cous
(Prep Time: 20 MIN │ Total Time: 45 MIN │ Servings: 4)

A delightful recipe for the colder months. You can use the vegetables in this recipe or any that you have on hand. Serve this dish with a fresh green salad.

Ingredients:
- 2 large Zucchini, chopped
- 1 large Yellow Squash, chopped
- 1 large Carrot, chopped
- 1 Sweet Potato, peeled and chopped
- 1 Red Onion, chopped
- 2 Roma Tomatoes, chopped
- 3 cloves Garlic
- 2 tbsp Olive Oil
- Salt and Pepper to taste
- 2 cups Cous Cous, cooked
- 1 Lemon juiced

Directions:
1. Preheat the oven to 375º F and line a baking sheet with parchment paper.
2. In a large mixing bowl, toss together the vegetables, garlic, oil, salt and pepper.
3. Arrange the vegetables on the baking sheet in a single layer (use 2 if necessary).
4. Place the baking sheet(s) in the oven and roast for 25 minutes. After 10 minutes, remove the garlic cloves and stir the remaining vegetables.
5. To serve, mince the garlic and sprinkle of the vegetables, then stir. Fill a serving bowl with a portion of cous cous, then top with roasted vegetables, and a sprinkle of lemon juice.

53. Buddha Bowl
(Prep Time: 15 MIN │Total Time: 30 MIN │Servings: 4)

Buddha bowls are fun because they are customizable. Add as much or as little of each ingredient as you like. You can exchange the tofu for edamame for a little variety with this dish.

Ingredients:
- 4 cups Spinach
- 2 cups Edamame
- 1 cup Red Cabbage, shredded
- 1 cup Carrots, shredded
- 1 cup Cucumber, julienned
- 1 cup Cherry Tomatoes, halved
- 1 cup Snow peas
- 1 cup Beets Shredded
- 1Red Bell, julienned
- 4 small Red Radishes, sliced into rounds
- 1 Lime, quartered
- Salt and Pepper to taste

Directions:
1. Assemble your bowl by placing 1 cup of spinach at the bottom of a medium sized serving bowl. Place a serving of each of the vegetables on top of the spinach in sections. Continue until all vegetables are nicely arranged over the spinach.
2. Sprinkle the juice of 1 lime quarter over the bowl with and then drizzle with Sriracha before serving.

54. White Chili
(Prep Time: 15 MIN │ Total Time: 45 MIN │ Servings: 6)

This white chili is full of velvety beans, a garlicy base and a delicious blend of spices. Try it with a side of tortilla chips or top it with some creamy avocado!

Ingredients:
- 1 tbsp Olive Oil
- 2 (20 oz) cans Young Jackfruit, drained and rinsed
- 1 medium Onion, chopped
- 1 clove Garlic, minced
- 1/8 teaspoon Ground Cloves
- 2 tsp Ground Cumin
- 1/4 teaspoon Cayenne Pepper
- 1 1/2 teaspoons dried oregano
- 2 Jalapenos, chopped
- 1 Serrano Pepper, chopped
- 2 (15-ounce) cans White Beans, drained and rinsed
- 3 cups Vegetable Stock
- Salt and Pepper to taste

Directions:
1. Heat the oil in large pot over medium heat. Place the jackfruit into the pot and sauté for 5 minutes. Add the onion and cook for 2 more minutes.
2. Place the garlic, cloves, cumin, cayenne, and oregano into the pot and stir intermittently for 2 minutes. Add the peppers and cook for 2 more minutes.
3. Pour in the beans, vegetable stock, and the season to taste with salt and pepper.
4. Simmer for about 15 more minutes or until the chili has thickened. Serve hot with tortilla chips.

55. Sesame Soba Noodles
(Prep Time: 15 MIN │Total Time: 40 MIN │Servings: 4)

These zesty noodles get their flavor from the aromatic sesame oil and the generous portion of white and black sesame seeds that grace the top.

Ingredients:
- 1 tbsp Vegetable Oil
- 2 cups Napa Cabbage, shredded
- 2 cups Snow Peas
- 2 cups Carrots, shredded
- 4 servings Soba Noodles, cooked
- 1 tbsp Sesame Oil
- 1 tsp Rice Wine Vinegar
- 2 tbsp Soy Sauce
- 2 tbsp Water
- 1 tbsp Maple Syrup
- 1 tbsp White Sesame Seeds
- 1 tbsp Black Sesame Seeds

Directions:
1. Heat the oil in a large skillet over high heat. Stir fry the cabbage, snow peas, and carrots for about 3 minutes.   Add the soba noodles and stir fry for 2 more minutes.   Reduce the heat to low.
2. In a small bowl, whisk together the sesame oil, soy sauce, water, and maple syrup. Pour the sauce into the skillet and stir fry until the liquid is fully absorbed.
3. To serve, place the noodles into a serving bowl and then top with a generous portion of sesame seeds.

56. Chickpea Pasta with Spinach Pesto and Sundried Tomatoes
(Prep Time: 20 MIN │ Total Time: 35 MIN │ Servings: 4)

Chickpea pasta is a great source of protein and makes an excellent gluten free pasta. This pasta usually cooks faster than traditionally pasta so keep an eye on it!

Ingredients:
- 2 cups packed Spinach
- 2 cloves Garlic
- ¼ cup Pine Nuts
- 2/3 cups Olive Oil
- ½ cup cashews, soaked overnight and drained
- 2 tbsp fresh Lemon Juice
- 4 servings Chickpea Spaghetti, cooked
- 1 tsp Vegetable Oil
- ¼ cup Sundried Tomatoes, julienned

Directions:
1. To make the pesto, place the spinach, garlic, pine nuts, olive oil, cashews, and lemon juice into a blender. Pulse on high until the mixture is smooth.
2. In a large skillet over medium heat, sauté the sundried tomatoes for 2 minutes and then add the chickpea pasta and pesto sauce.
3. Toss to fully coat the pasta with pesto and then serve hot.

57. Mushroom Wild Rice
(Prep Time: 10 MIN │ Total Time: 35 MIN │ Servings: 4)

This earthy combo is creamy, savory, and incredibly delicious. Its versatile enough to add in some of your favorite veggies if you so desire. It also saves well so pack up some leftovers to take for lunch!

Ingredients:
- 2 tbsp Vegetable Oil
- ¼ cup Red Onion, chopped
- 2 cups Cremini Mushrooms, chopped
- 2 cloves Garlic, chopped
- 2 sprigs fresh Oregano, stems removed, chopped
- 1 ½ cups Wild Rice
- 3 cups Vegetable Stock
- Salt and Pepper to taste

Directions:
1. Heat the oil in a large pot over medium heat. Sauté the onion and mushrooms for 3 minutes then add the garlic and sauté for two more minutes.
2. Place the oregano into the pot and then add the rice, vegetable stock and season to taste with salt and pepper.
3. Bring the mixture to a simmer and then cover the pot with a lid. Simmer for 20 minutes or until the liquid has absorbed.
4. Allow the rice to rest for 5 minutes before fluffing with a fork. Serve hot.

58. Fajita Veggie Bowl
(Prep Time: 10 MIN │Total Time: 25 MIN │Servings: 4)

This recipe works best with a cast iron skillet. It will roast your veggies just right for that yummy fajita flare. Serve with flour tortillas and your favorite fajita toppings.

Ingredients:
- 2 tbsp Vegetable Oil
- 2 cups Shiitake Mushrooms, julienned
- 1 Onion, julienned
- 2 Red Bell Pepper, seeded and julienned
- 2 Green Bell Pepper, seeded and julienned
- 1 tbsp Ground Cumin
- 1 tbsp Chili Powder
- 1 tsp Garlic Powder
- Salt and Pepper to taste
- 8 Flour Tortillas
- Vegan Sour Cream (optional)
- Shredded Vegan Cheese (optional)

Directions:
1. Preheat the oven to 425º F prepare your cast iron skillet or line a baking sheet with parchment paper.
2. In a large bowl over medium heat, toss together the vegetable oil, mushrooms, onion, bell peppers, cumin, chili powder, garlic powder, salt, and pepper.
3. Arrange the veggies in one layer on the bottom of the cast iron skillet or baking sheet. Place them into the oven for 10 minutes, stir the vegetables halfway through.
4. Serve fajita veggies on a flour tortilla with sour cream and shredded cheese or any of your favorite fajita toppings.

59. One Pot Quinoa with Tomatoes and Kale
(Prep Time: 5 MIN │ Total Time: 35 MIN │ Servings: 4)

This is a super easy recipe that is great for lunch or dinner. Just throw everything in the pot and let it simmer. Quinoa is a great protein source for vegans and with the added boost from kale, you'll feel satiated and satisfied until your next meal!

Ingredients:
- 1 tbsp Vegetable Oil
- ¼ cup Onion, thinly sliced
- 2 cups Kale, chopped
- 1 clove Garlic, minced
- 1 Tomato, chopped
- 1 ½ cups Quinoa
- 3 cups Vegetable Stock
- Salt and Pepper to taste

Directions:
1. Heat the oil in a large pot over medium heat. Sauté the onions for 2 minutes then add the kale. Cook for 2 more minutes, stirring occasionally.
2. Add the garlic, tomato, quinoa, and vegetable stock then stir. Season with salt and pepper and then place a lid on the pot.
3. Simmer for 20 minutes or until the liquid has absorbed. Allow the quinoa to rest for 5 minutes before serving.

60. Broccoli and Fettuccini in White Wine Sauce
(Prep Time: 10 MIN | Total Time: 35 MIN | Servings: 4)

A delicious pasta to prepare for your next dinner guests. This flavorful dish has a delicious crunch from the broccoli that is cooked al dente.

Ingredients:
- 1 tbsp Vegetable Oil
- 2 cups Broccoli Florets
- 2 cloves Garlic, Minced
- 1 cup Cherry Tomatoes, halved
- ¼ cup Dry White Wine
- Salt and Pepper to taste
- 1 tbsp Vegan Butter
- 4 servings Fettuccini Pasta, cooked

Directions:
1. Heat the oil in a large skillet over medium heat. Sauté the broccoli for 3 minutes then reduce the heat to low and add the garlic, tomatoes, and wine. Stir and then season with salt and pepper.
2. Allow the mixture to simmer until the liquid has reduced by half, about 5 minutes. Add the vegan butter and the fettuccini, toss to combine well and serve.

Appetizers and Side Dishes

61. Roasted Corn and Black Bean Dip
(Prep Time: 15 MIN │ Total Time: 25 MIN │ Servings: 6)

This one is a hit! Keep your guests satisfied and hungry for more flavor with this easy, and delicious appetizer. It is a great gluten free option for dinner guests.

Ingredients:
- 2 cups Corn, frozen
- 1 Onion, finely chopped
- 2 cloves Garlic, minced
- 2 cups Kale, finely chopped
- 1 (15 ounce) can Black Beans, drained and rinsed
- ¼ cup Water
- 1 tbsp, Lime Juice
- Salt and Pepper to taste

Directions:
1. Preheat the oven to 375° F, then line a baking sheet with parchment paper. Arrange the corn on the baking sheet and place in the oven for 10 minutes, stir once halfway through.
2. Meanwhile, heat the oil in a medium sized pot over medium heat. Sauté the onion and garlic for 1 minute then add the water, lime juice and season with salt and pepper.
3. Allow the mixture to simmer until the corn has finished roasting. Stir the corn into the pot and combine well.
4. Serve with tortilla chips

62. Roasted Carrot Hummus
(Prep Time: 20 MIN | Total Time: 30 MIN | Servings: 6)

Revive regular old hummus with this roasted root vegetable. The carrot adds an earthy flavor to bright and tangy hummus. Dip veggies or pita into or you can even use it as a sandwich spread!

Ingredients:
- 1 tbsp Vegetable Oil
- 2 medium sized Carrots, rough chopped
- 1 (15 oz) can Chickpeas, drained and rinsed
- 2 tbsp Lemon Juice
- 2 cloves Garlic, minced
- 1 tbsp Tahini
- 2 tbsp Water
- 2 tbsp Olive Oil
- Salt and Pepper to taste

Directions:
1. Preheat the oven to 375° F then line a baking sheet with parchment paper. Toss the carrots in the vegetable oil and season with a pinch of salt and pepper. Place the carrots in the oven and roast for 15 minutes, turning half way through.
2. Meanwhile, place the remaining ingredients into a food processor. When the carrots are done roasting add them into the blender with the mixture and blend on high until smooth.
3. Serve with vegetables or pita bread

63. Sundried Tomato Cashew Cheese Spread
(Prep Time: 10 MIN │ Total Time: 20 MIN │ Servings: 6)

These spread is zesty, savory, and the perfect accompaniment to a crusty French baguette. This spread also tasted great on sandwich, or in a wrap.

Ingredients:

- 1 cup Cashews, soaked overnight and drained
- 1/2 cup Red Bell Pepper, chopped
- 1 clove Garlic, chopped
- 2 tbsp fresh Lemon Juice
- 1/4 tsp Smoked Paprika
- Dash of Cayenne Pepper
- Salt and Pepper to taste
- 2 French Baguettes, sliced and toasted

Directions:

1. Place all of the ingredients except for the baguette into a food processor. Blend on high until smooth. Mixture will be thick.
2. Serve with toasted baguette.

64. Mango Guacamole
(Prep Time: 25 MIN │ Total Time: 30 MIN │ Servings: 2)

Mangoes in guacamole are the best think you haven't tried yet. You may never eat guacamole the same way again. Serve this guac with your favorite tortilla chips.

Ingredients:
- 4 Avocados, peeled, seeded, and chopped
- 1 Jalapeno Pepper, minced
- 1 clove Garlic, minced
- 1 cup Red Onion, finely chopped
- 1 cup Tomato, finely chopped
- ½ cup fresh Cilantro, stems removed and finely chopped
- 1 Lime, juiced
- 2 tbsp Olive Oil
- 1 cup Mangoes, small diced
- Salt and Pepper to taste

Directions:
1. In a small bowl, mash the avocados. Stir in the remaining ingredients and mix until well combined.
2. Serve with tortilla chips.

65. Fiesta Stuffed Potatoes
(Prep Time: 5 MIN │ Total Time: 35 MIN │ Servings: 6)

Bring these delicious potatoes to your next party or pot luck. Or use them as an accompaniment on Taco Tuesday! They are simple to make and have a ton of flavor.

Ingredients:
- 12 small Red Potatoes
- 1 (15 oz) can Black Beans, drained and rinsed
- 1 (15 oz) can Sweet Corn Kernels, drained
- 1 (8 oz) can Diced Tomatoes
- Salt and Pepper to taste
- 2 Avocados, peeled, seeded, and thinly sliced
- ¼ cup fresh Cilantro, chopped
- 2 tbsp fresh Lime Juice

Directions:
1. Place the potatoes into a large pot and then fill it with water. Bring the pot to a boil and cook for 6 minutes or until softened. Remove the potatoes from the pot and allow to cool.
2. In a medium sized bowl, combine the black beans, corn, and tomatoes. Season with salt and pepper.
3. Preheat the oven to 375° F and line a baking sheet with parchment paper. Once the potatoes have cooled, split them open and mash the insides a bit to make room for the stuffing. Stuff each potato with the bean mixture and then place them in the oven to bake for 15 minutes.
4. Remove the stuffed potatoes from the oven and place them on a serving tray. Top each potato with avocado slices, cilantro and a squeeze of lime juice.

66. Ginger Tofu Lettuce Cups
(Prep Time: 15 MIN │ Total Time: 35 MIN │ Servings: 4)

A nice and light appetizer with a fresh, zingy flavor. The tofu is combined with a delicious ginger sauce and then simmered with carrots and water chestnuts for a delicious crunch.

Ingredients:
- 1-inch fresh Ginger, grated
- 3 tbsp, Soy Sauce
- 2 tbsp Water
- 1 Lime, juiced
- 2 tbsp Maple Syrup
- 2 tbsp Vegetable Oil
- 1 block Tofu, drained and pressed
- 1 (2 oz) can Water Chestnuts, drained and fine chopped
- 1 large Carrot, shredded
- 2 heads Romaine Lettuce, leaves separated

Directions:
1. In a small bowl, whisk together the ginger, soy sauce, water, lime juice, and maples syrup. Set aside.
2. Heat the oil in large skillet over medium heat. Crumble the tofu as you add it to the skillet and sauté for 3 minutes. Add in the water chestnuts and carrots then cook for another 3 minutes.
3. Pour the ginger - soy sauce mixture into the skillet with the tofu. Cook for 2 more minutes and then remove from the heat.
4. Serve the ginger tofu with romaine lettuce leaves.

67. Eggplant Pinwheels
(Prep Time: 20 MIN | Total Time: 35 MIN | Servings: 6)

Eggplant is paired with an herbaceous olive mixture then rolled up in flour tortillas with tomatoes and kale. A perfect finger food for your next fling.

Ingredients:
- 1 cup Mixed Olives
- 1 tsp Dried Oregano
- ½ tsp Dried Thyme
- 1 tsp Dried Parsley
- 2 tbsp Olive Oil
- 1 clove Garlic
- 1 tbsp Lemon Juice
- 1 large Eggplant, thinly sliced
- 1 large Tomato, thinly sliced into rounds
- 12 whole Kale Leaves
- 4 large Flour Tortillas

Directions:
1. Place the olives, oregano, thyme, parsley, olive oil, garlic, and lemon juice into a food processor and pulse to combine well.
2. Lay out the flour tortillas and spread the olive mixture evenly amongst them. Place a few slices of eggplant on top of the olive mixture, then a few leaves of kale, followed by a few slices of tomato.
3. Take one end of the tortilla and roll it up. Make slices down the length of the rolled tortilla to create pinwheel shapes.
4. Serve the pinwheels at room temperature on a large platter.

68. Garlicky Basil Mushrooms
(Prep Time: 10 MIN │Total Time: 25 MIN │Servings: 4)

These mushrooms are a perfect side dish or a delicious appetizer for any meal. A total breeze to prepare and

Ingredients:
- 1 tbsp Vegetable Oil
- 2 lb Portobello Mushrooms, thinly sliced
- 2 cloves Garlic, minced
- Salt and Pepper to taste
- 2 tbsp of Dry white wine
- 2 tbsp fresh Basil, finely chopped

Directions:
1. Heat the oil in a large skillet over medium heat and sauté the mushrooms for 3 minutes. Add the garlic and sauté for 2 more minutes. Season with salt and pepper.
2. Turn the temperature to low and pour in the white wine. Simmer for 3 – 4 minutes or until the sauce thickened. Stir in the basil and serve hot.

69. Roasted Brussels Sprouts
(Prep Time: 20 MIN │Total Time: 50 MIN │Servings: 6)

These roasted sprouts are divine! Made simply with just three ingredients tossed together with the Brussels Sprouts to enhance their earthy flavor. Try them alone or as an accompaniment to a delish meal!

Ingredients:
- 2 ½ cups Brussels sprouts, sliced in half
- 1 tbsp Olive oil
- Sea Salt to taste
- Freshly Cracked Black Pepper to taste

Directions:
1. Preheat the oven to 375° F and line a baking sheet with parchment paper.
2. In a large mixing bowl, toss together all of the ingredients and then place them in a single layer on the prepared baking sheet.
3. Roast for 20 minutes, stirring intermittently then remove from the oven and allow to rest for 5 minutes before serving.

70. Green Beans Almondine
(Prep Time: 5 MIN │Total Time: 15 MIN │Servings: 4)

A French classic. These green beans are flavorful with a nice touch of toasted almonds. They taste great with a meatless loaf or try them in your Buddha bowl!

Ingredients:
- 1 tbsp Vegetable Oil
- 1 lb French Cut Green Beans
- Salt and Pepper to taste
- 1 tbsp Vegan Butter
- 3 tbsp Almond Flakes

Directions:
1. Warm the oil in a large skillet over medium heat then sauté them for 2 minutes. Reduce the heat and cover the green beans with a lid or a piece of foil. Cook for 5 more minutes, stirring occasionally.
2. Transfer the green beans to a serving plate and place the butter in the skillet. Once melted place the almond flakes in the butter and sauté for about 1 minute, taking care not to burn them. Top the green beans with the toasted almonds and serve.

71. Balsamic Roasted Acorn Squash
(Prep Time: 10 MIN │Total Time: 40 MIN │Servings: 4)

These roasted acorn squash are perfectly caramelized and enticingly sweet. Simply toss the squash in the balsamic mixture and roast to perfection.

Ingredients:
- 2 Acorn Squash, seeds removed
- 2 tbsp Olive Oil
- 1 tbsp Balsamic Vinegar
- 1 tsp Dried Oregano
- Salt and Pepper to taste

Directions:
1. Preheat the oven to 375° F and line a baking sheet with parchment paper.
2. Cut the acorn squash into ¼ inch wide slices. In a medium sized bowl, whisk together the remaining ingredients and then toss the acorn squash in the mixture to fully coat.
3. Arrange the squash onto the prepared baking sheet in one layer. Place squash into the oven and bake for about 20 -30 minutes, flipping halfway through. Remove the squash from the oven when it is tender to the touch.

72. Sautéed Kale and Red Onions
(Prep Time: 5 MIN │Total Time: 15 MIN │Servings: 4)

This side dish is so tasty that you can eat it all by itself! Onions are sautéed along with hearty kale and just a few other ingredients in this healthy and delicious dish.

Ingredients:
- 1 tbsp Vegetable Oil
- 2 tbsp Water
- 1 Onion, thinly sliced
- 4 cups Kale, chopped
- Salt and Pepper to taste
- ¼ cup Vegetable Stock

Directions:
1. Heat the oil in a large pot over low heat. Add the onions and sauté for 3 minutes. Pour in the water and continue to cook for 3 or 4 more minutes.
2. Add the remaining ingredients and stir well. Place a lid or aluminum foil over the pot and cook for 5 minutes.
3. Remove the lid, stir the kale mixture and then serve hot.

73. Root Vegetable Roast
(Prep Time: 10 MIN │ Total Time: 40 MIN │ Servings: 4)

Root vegetables have so much flavor! These roasted beauties will light up any dish you pair them with. They are slightly charred, deliciously caramelized, and perfectly tender.

Ingredients:
- 1 large Sweet Potato, medium diced
- 2 Parsnips, medium diced
- 2 Turnips, medium diced
- 6 small sun chokes, sliced in half
- 1 Rutabaga, medium diced
- 2 tbsp Vegetable Oil
- 2 sprigs Thyme
- ¼ tsp Garlic Powder
- Salt and Pepper to taste
- Fresh Lemon Juice as needed

Directions:
1. Preheat the oven to 375° F and line a baking sheet with parchment paper.
2. In a large mixing bowl, toss together all of the ingredients except for the lemon juice. Arrange the root vegetables in one layer on the baking sheet and place in the oven for 30 minutes, flipping half way through.
3. Remove the vegetables when they are tender to the touch. Sprinkle them with fresh lemon juice before serving.

74. Yellow Rice
(Prep Time: 5 MIN │Total Time: 40 MIN │Servings: 4)

This is a colorful addition to any meal. It gets it's beautiful, yellow hue from turmeric, an ancient ayurvedic spice. Try this rice as a side to curried beans or any other dish that you choose.

Ingredients:
- 1 tbsp Olive Oil
- ¼ cup Onion, finely chopped
- 2 tsp Turmeric Powder
- 1 cup Brown Basmati Rice
- 1 cup Water
- 1 cup Coconut Milk
- Salt and Pepper to taste

Directions:
1. Heat the oil in a medium sized pot over medium heat. Sauté the onion and turmeric for 2 minutes then add the remaining ingredients.
2. Place the lid on the pot and cook for 30 minutes or until all of the liquid is absorbed. Allow to rest for 5 minutes then fluff with a fork before serving.

75. Burmese Potatoes
(Prep Time: 10 MIN │ Total Time: 30 MIN │ Servings: 4)

These curried potatoes are tender, flavorful, and simple to make. The Burmese curry flavor comes bursting through with every bite. Pair them with greens or a mushroom dish for a complete meal.

Ingredients:
- ¼ cup Vegetable Oil
- 1 large Onion, finely chopped
- 1 clove Garlic, minced
- ½ inch thumb, Ginger, minced
- 1 tsp. Ground Turmeric
- 1 tsp. Cayenne
- 4 large Red Potatoes, large diced
- ½ cup Water

Directions:
1. Heat the oil in a large pot over medium heat. Sauté the onion, garlic, ginger, turmeric, and cayenne for 2 minutes. Stir in the potatoes and water.
2. Reduce the heat to a simmer then cover the pot with a lid or aluminum foil.   Cook for 10 more minutes or until the potatoes tender. Serve hot.

Dressings and Sauces

76. Vegan Ranch
(Prep Time: 15 MIN │ Total Time: 15 MIN │ Servings: 16)

The ultimate sauce. It goes on salads and grain bowls or serves as the perfect dip for buffalo cauliflower and fried zucchini. The possibilities are endless and absolutely delicious.

Ingredients:
- 1 cup Vegan Mayonnaise
- ½ cup Unsweetened Plant Milk
- 2 tsp Lemon Juice
- ½ tsp Onion Powder
- ½ tsp Garlic Powder
- ¼ tsp Black Pepper
- 1 tbsp dill, chopped
- 2 tsp parsley, chopped

Directions:
Place all of the ingredients into a medium sized bowl and then whisk until combined. Chill for 2 hours before serving.

77. Lemon Tahini
(Prep Time: 5 MIN | Total Time: 5 MIN | Servings: 4)

Drizzle it on your falafel, your roasted veggies or toss it with your kale salad or spread it on your wrap. Tahini is made from ground sesame seeds but only has a mild sesame flavor.

Ingredients:
- 1 cup Tahini
- 1 Lemon, juiced
- 2 tbsp Water
- Salt and Pepper to taste

Directions:
1. Place all of the ingredients into a medium sized bowl and then whisk until combined. Chill for 2 hours before serving.

78. Nacho Cheese Sauce
(Prep Time: 15 MIN │ Total Time: 25 MIN │ Servings: 6)

Drizzle this "cheese" on nachos, dip it with tortilla chips or toss it with pasta for a zesty, plant-based mac 'n cheese. The sauce is quick and easy to make yet packs a ton of flavor. You're gonna love it!

Ingredients:
- 2 cups White Potatoes, chopped and boiled
- 3/4 cups Carrots chopped and boiled
- 1 clove Garlic, chopped
- 1/3 cup Vegetable oil
- 1/3 cup Water
- 1 tbsp Lemon Juice
- 1 tbsp Pickled Jalapenos
- Salt and Pepper to taste

Directions:
1. Place all of the ingredients into a high speed blender. Process on high until smooth. If so desired, heat the sauce in a medium sized pot over low heat before serving.

79. Thai Peanut Sauce
(Prep Time: 15 MIN │Total Time: 15 MIN │Servings: 4)

Perfect for all things Asian Cuisine. This sauce tastes great over a Buddha bowl or a delicious spinach salad. It is also the perfect companion for spring rolls. It's so easy to make and packed full of protein.

Ingredients:
- ½ cup Creamy Peanut Butter
- ¾ cup Coconut Milk
- 2 tbsp Soy Sauce
- 2 tbsp Apple Cider Vinegar
- 1 small Thai Chili, minced (optional)
- 1 tbsp Maple Syrup
- Salt and Pepper to taste

Directions:
1. Combine all of the ingredients into a medium sized bowl. Whisk to combine until smooth the serve.

80. Creamy Avocado Dressing
(Prep Time: 15 MIN │Total Time: 15 MIN │Servings: 4)

A creamy dressing for salads, and dips. Try roasting some thick cut potatoes and then prepare this dressing to dip them in. The combination is heavenly and so simple to create.

Ingredients:
- 2 Avocado peeled and pitted
- ¼ large fresh Parsley, chopped
- ¼ cup fresh Cilantro leaves loosely packed
- ¼ cup fresh Chives loosely packed
- 2 tbsp Lemon Juice
- ¼ Red Onion, chopped
- 1 clove Garlic, chopped
- Salt and Pepper to taste

Directions:
1. Place all of the ingredients into a blender and then process on high until smooth. Refrigerate for 2 hours before serving.

81. Balsamic Vinaigrette
(Prep Time: 5 MIN │Total Time: 5 MIN │Servings: 6)

This is a classic dressing that works for more than just salads. Try marinating potatoes in this dressing before roasting them.   You can also cook this dressing down and create a reduction to drizzle over grilled eggplant.

Ingredients:
- ½ cup Olive Oil
- ¼ cup Balsamic Vinegar
- 1 tbsp Dijon Mustard
- 1 tbsp Maple Syrup
- ¼ tsp Garlic Powder
- Salt and Pepper to taste

Directions:
1. Place all of the ingredients into a container with a secure lid. Shake the contents until well combined.

82. Holiday Hemp
(Prep Time: 10 MIN | Total Time: 10 MIN | Servings: 6)

The flavor of cranberries, orange and spices come together for this creamy dressing. Try it on top of stuffing or drizzle it over a wrap. Also makes a great dip for roasted root vegetables.

Ingredients:
- 1 cup Cranberries
- ¼ cup Hemp Seeds
- 2 tbsp Water
- 1 Orange, Juiced
- 1 dash Ground Cinnamon
- 1 dash Ground Ginger
- 1 tbsp Apple Cider Vinegar
- ¼ cup Olive Oil

Directions:
1. Place all of the ingredients into a container with a secure lid. Shake the contents until well combined.

83. Raspberry Vinaigrette
(Prep Time: 5 MIN | Total Time: 5 MIN | Servings: 6)

This dressing is sweet and mildly tangy. Toss it with a big salad for a bright and flavorful combination. This dressing is easy to make ahead of time and pack for a potluck.

Ingredients:
- 1 cup fresh Raspberries
- ½ cup Water
- ¼ cup Apple cider Vinegar
- 2 tbsp Agave Nectar
- Salt and Pepper to taste

Directions:
1. Place all of the ingredients into a container with a secure lid. Shake the contents until well combined.

84. Maple Mustard Sauce
(Prep Time: 5 MIN │Total Time: 5 MIN │Servings: 6)

A vegan answer to honey mustard. Just three simple ingredients to make this amazing dressing. This sauce tastes amazing on roasted cauliflower and makes a tasty accompaniment to your grain bowl.

Ingredients:
- ½ cup Yellow Mustard
- ¼ cup Maple Syrup
- 1 tsp Lemon Juice

Directions:
1. Place the ingredients into a bowl and whisk until well combined.

85. Basil Pistachio Dressing
(Prep Time: 10 MIN │Total Time: 10 MIN │Servings: 4)

This sauce tastes great with grain bowls ad Buddha bowls but the fun doesn't have to stop there! Try it over zoodles with sundried tomatoes or spread it on top of bread for a midday snack.

Ingredients:
- 1 Avocado, peeled, pitted, and chopped
- ¼ cup fresh Basil
- ¼ cup fresh Cilantro
- 1 Lemon, juiced
- ¼ Red Onion, roughly chopped
- 1 clove Garlic, roughly chopped
- Salt and Pepper to taste

Directions:
1. Place all of the ingredients into a high speed blender and process until smooth.

86. Sesame Miso
(Prep Time: 5 MIN │Total Time: 5 MIN │Servings: 4)

A wonderful dip for fried tofu or a great garnish to a Buddha bowl. This dressing only has 5 ingredients but you won't believe it. It's so flavorful and so easy.

Ingredients:
- 1 tsp Sesame Oil
- 2 tbsp Miso Paste
- ¼ cup water
- ¼ cup Olive Oil
- 1 tbsp Maple Syrup

Directions:
1. Place all of the ingredients in a medium sized mixing bowl. Whisk until well combined.

87. Creamy Dill Dressing
(Prep Time: 10 MIN │Total Time: 10 MIN │Servings: 4)

Dill is such a refreshing flavor. Pour this dressing over roasted potatoes, add it to your grain bowl, or use it as a salad dressing to coat tender greens in a bowl full of bright fruits and vegetables.

Ingredients:
- 1 cup Cashews, soaked overnight and drained
- ¼ cup fresh Dill
- 1 clove Garlic
- ¼ cup Water
- ¼ cup Olive Oil
- 2 tbsp Lemon Juice

Directions:
1. Place all of the ingredients into a high speed blender and process on high until smooth.

88. Carrot Ginger Dressing
(Prep Time: 10 MIN │Total Time: 10 MIN │Servings: 6)

The bite of ginger makes this dressing very special. Of course it tastes wonderful with any Asian inspired dis. Try marinating butternut squash in the dressing for one hour and then roast to perfection.

Ingredients:
- ¼ cup Olive Oil
- 1 tsp Sesame Oil
- ¼ cup Apple Cider Vinegar
- 1 medium Carrot, peeled and chopped
- 1 inch thumb Ginger, peeled and chopped
- 2 tbsp Maple Syrup
- 1 tbsp Soy Sauce

Directions:
1. Place all of the ingredients into a bowl and whisk together until combined.

89. Cilantro Lime
(Prep Time: 5 MIN │Total Time: 5 MIN │Servings: 2)

Cilantro and lime are a classic combination that pairs well with many world flavors. From Latin, to Mediterranean, African, and Asian, these flavors will make any dish pop.

Ingredients:
- ½ cup fresh Cilantro, chopped
- ½ cup Olive Oil
- 2 Limes, Juiced
- ½ tbsp Agave

Directions:
1. Place the ingredients into a high speed blender and process on high until smooth.

90. Creamy Garlic Sauce
(Prep Time: 5 MIN │Total Time: 5 MIN │Servings: 4)

Out to prove that Garlic goes with everything? Try this sauce! It's amazing on pizza, as a veggie dip, tossed on a salad, or served over asparagus. Feel free to spice it up with a small green chili.

Ingredients:
- 1 cup Hemp Seeds
- ½ cup Water
- 2 tsp Lemon Juice
- 2 cloves Garlic, chopped
- Salt and Pepper to taste

Directions:
1. Place the ingredients into a high speed blender and process on high until smooth.

Salads and Snacks

91. Quinoa Salad with Chickpeas and Avocado
(Prep Time: 20 MIN │ Total Time: 30 MIN │ Servings: 4)

A refreshing and filling salad that is perfect for a summer day. This salad travels well so take leftovers for lunch time at work or school. You'll love the creamy avocados mixed with the chewy quinoa.

Ingredients:
- 1 (15 oz) can Chickpeas, drained and rinsed
- 2 Avocados, peeled, pitted, and diced
- 2 cups Quinoa, cooked and cooled
- 2 tbsp Parsley, chopped
- ¼ cup Cilantro, chopped
- 2 tsp Lemon juice
- 1 cup Cherry Tomatoes, sliced in half
- Salt and Pepper to taste

Directions:
1. Toss the ingredients together in a large mixing bowl and then serve.

92. Seeds and Nuts
(Prep Time: 5 MIN │Total Time: 15 MIN │Servings: 4)

This is a delicious snack and protein pick me up. You'll love how simple it is to make and how versatile the recipe is. Toss in other nuts or dried fruits as you wish. Also try these as a salad topper!

Ingredients:
- ¼ tsp Dried Parsley
- ½ tsp Smoked Paprika
- ¼ tsp Garlic Powder
- ¼ tsp Sea Salt
- ½ cup Cashew Pieces
- ½ cup Slivered Almonds
- ½ cup Pepitas
- ½ cup Sunflower Seeds

Directions:
1. In a small bowl, combine the herbs and spices. Set aside.
2. Place the nuts and seeds into a large skillet over low heat. Toss several times a minute to avoid burning. Continue to cook for about 3 minutes, or until they are glistening.
3. Transfer to a paper towel and immediately sprinkle with the seasoning mix.   Allow to cool for 5 minutes before serving.

93. Almond Butter Rolls
(Prep Time: 5 MIN │ Total Time: 10 MIN │ Servings: 4)

These are an amazing snack for the versatility and portability. Use any fruit that you have in the fridge. Wrap a few of the rolls in foil and then carry them with you for a quick pick me up throughout the day.

Ingredients:
- 4 Whole Wheat Tortillas
- ¼ cup Almond Butter
- ½ cup Strawberries, sliced
- 1 Banana, sliced into coins
- ¼ cup Cacao Nibs

Directions:
1. Place a tortilla on a flat surface. Spread 1 tbsp of almond butter on top then add a few slices of banana and strawberry on the tortilla then roll it up. Seal the end of the tortilla with a little more nut butter and then serve.

94. Avocado Toast
(Prep Time: 5 MIN │Total Time: 10 MIN │Servings: 2)

Creamy avocado on top of crunchy bread. OMG! No wonder it is a hit amongst vegans and non-vegans alike. Add tomatoes or microgreens to bring a little variety to this recipe.

Ingredients:
- 2 Avocados, peeled, pitted, and sliced into strips
- 4 Slices Rustic Whole Wheat Bread, sliced and toasted
- Salt, Pepper, and Red Pepper Flakes to taste
- 1 tsp Olive Oil

Directions:
1. Place the sliced avocados on top of the toasted bread then season with salt pepper and red pepper flakes. Garnish with a drizzle of olive oil.

95. Pink Banana Nicecream
(Prep Time: 10 MIN | Total Time: 15 MIN | Servings: 2)

When did ice cream become healthy? When vegans started blending up frozen bananas, that's when! Try this delicious combo with chocolate sauce or toasted almonds on top.

Ingredients:
- 4 Bananas, frozen
- 1 cup Raspberries, frozen
- ¼ cup Almond Flakes
- ¼ cup Vegan Chocolate Chips

Directions:
1. Place frozen bananas and raspberries into a food processor. Pulse until smooth, about 5 minutes.

96. Chocolate Cherry Smoothie
(Prep Time: 5 MIN │Total Time: 5 MIN │Servings: 4)

With just a few simple ingredients you can enjoy this sweet, tasty, and delicious treat, guilt free, any time of the day.

Ingredients:
- 2 cups Unsweetened Plant Milk
- 1 lb frozen Cherries, pitted
- ¼ cup Cacao Powder
- ¼ cup Hemp Seeds

Directions:
1. Place all of the ingredients into a high speed blender and process until smooth.

97. Green Salad
(Prep Time: 15 MIN │Total Time: 15 MIN │Servings: 4)

This salad is full of fiber and delicious nutrients that your body needs to be healthy and strong. Try it with the Creamy Dill dressing from this book.

Ingredients:
- 2 heads Romaine, chopped
- 2 cups Baby Spinach
- 1 cup Edamame
- 1 Green Bell Pepper, seeded and julienned
- 1 Avocado, peeled, pitted and julienned
- 1 cup Broccoli Florets

Directions:
1. In a large salad bowl toss together all of the ingredients. Drizzle with Creamy Dill dressing (found in this book) and toss once more before serving.

98. Cucumber Tomato Salad
(Prep Time: 15 MIN │ Total Time: 30 MIN │ Servings: 4)

This salad is fresh and tangy. Enjoy it on a hot summer's day for a bit of rehydration. You'll love this as a picnic dish or a wonderful addition to any potluck.

Ingredients:
- 4 Cucumber, peeled, seeded and diced
- 2 Tomatoes, diced
- 1 tbsp Apple Cider Vinegar
- 1 tbsp Olive Oil
- 1 tsp Cumin
- Salt and Pepper to taste

Directions:
1. In a large mixing bowl, combine all of the ingredients and allow to rest for at least 30 minutes prior to serving.

99. Apple and Kale Salad
(Prep Time: 15 MIN | Total Time: 15 MIN | Servings: 4)

Kale plays nicely with shredded apples in this simple salad recipe. Eat a salad like this a couple of times a week to kick your immune system into full gear! Try it with one of the dressings in the book, Maple Mustard perhaps?

Ingredients:
- 4 cups Kale, chopped
- 1 Apple, shredded
- ¼ cup Sunflower Seeds
- 2 tbsp Craisins
- ½ cup Cherry Tomatoes, halved
- Salt and Pepper to taste

Directions:
1. In a large mixing bowl, combine all of the ingredients together and then toss to mix well. Pair with one of the dressings from the book like Maple Mustard, Lemon Tahini, or Basil Pistachio.

100. Apple Nachos
(Prep Time: 20 MIN │Total Time: 20 MIN │Servings: 2)

This snack will satisfy your sweet tooth!   Crunchy apples are smothered with a raw vegan caramel sauce and topped with delicious vegan chocolate chips.

Ingredients:
- ½ cup Almond Butter
- 4 Dates, pitted (the stickiest you can find!)
- 1 tbsp Coconut Oil
- 3 Granny Smith Apples, cored and sliced into strips
- ¼ cup Vegan Chocolate Chips

Directions:
1. Place the almond butter, dates, and coconut oil into a food processor then blend on high until smooth.
2. Lay the apple slices flat on a plate and then drizzle with the caramel sauce.   Top with vegan chocolate chips to serve.

Printed in Great Britain
by Amazon